Charlotte Waterlow

teaches history at Browne and Nichols School in Cambridge, Massachusetts, and is the author of *Tribe, State and Community, India,* and *Europe 1945 to 1970.* A graduate of Cambridge University and a member of the Executive Committee of the United Nations' Association of Greater Boston and of the world federalists, her chief interest lies in promoting an understanding of the problems of poor countries.

D0872898

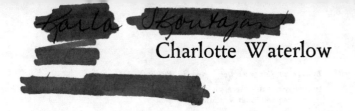

Charlotte Waterlow

SUPERPOWERS AND VICTIMS

The Outlook for World Community

A SPECTRUM BOOK

PRENTICE-HALL, INC., ENGLEWOOD CLIFFS, NEW JERSEY

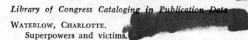

Library of Congress Cataloging in Publication Data

WATERLOW, CHARLOTTE.
  Superpowers and victims.

  (A Spectrum Book)
  Includes bibliographical references.
  1. Underdeveloped areas. I. Title.
HC59.7.W36   338.91′172′4   73–20466
ISBN 0–13–876227–9
ISBN 0–13–876219–8 (pbk.)

PRENTICE-HALL INTERNATIONAL, INC. (*London*)
PRENTICE-HALL OF AUSTRALIA PTY., LTD. (*Sydney*)
PRENTICE-HALL OF CANADA, LTD. (*Toronto*)
PRENTICE-HALL OF INDIA PRIVATE LIMITED (*New Delhi*)
PRENTICE-HALL OF JAPAN, INC. (*Tokyo*)

CONTENTS

v

PREFACE

I should like to express my gratitude to the following experts and friends who have given me advice and help concerning various parts of the book: the following officials of the Overseas Development Administration of the British Foreign and Commonwealth Relations Office: Mr. D. Victor Moore, Press Officer; Mr. B. J. Youngjohns, Advisor on Co-operatives; Mr. J. C. D. Lawrence, Advisor on Land Reform; Mr. P. J. Dyball Senior Press Officer, United Kingdom Atomic Energy Authority; Lord Wilberforce; Mr. Patrick Armstrong, Secretary to the Parliamentary Group for World Government in London; Sir George Deacon, Director of the National Institute of Oceanography in England; Miss Margaret Deacon; Sir Edward Warner, formerly British Ambassador in Tunisia; Professor John Waterlow, of the London School of Tropical Hygiene and Medicine; Sir Hugh Springer, Secretary-General of the Association of Commonwealth Universities; Mr. Harold Houghton, formerly Deputy Education Advisor to the British Colonial Office; Professor Frank Paish, formerly of the London School of Economics; Mr. Archibald Evans, formerly of the International Labor Office; Mrs. Hester Boothroyd, Under-Secretary in the British Treasury; Mr. Francis Boothroyd, Secretary of the Freedom from Hunger Campaign in England; Dr. Phyllis Martin, Lecturer on African History at the University of Indiana at Bloomington; Mr. Peter Tulloch, of the Overseas Development Institute, London; Miss Deborah Ainger, of the Intermediate Technology Group Ltd. London; Dr. Alan F. Guttmacher, President, Planned Parent World Population of New York; Mr. John Cairns of UNESCO; M. Pierre de Fontnouvelle, Information Officer at the International Monetary Fund; Mary Hynes; Mr. Arvind Sharma, formerly of the Indian Administrative Service; Dr. Carl Gotsch of the Department of Economics of Harvard University, and the Rev. Norman Farimelli, of the Boston Industrial Mission.

I should like especially to thank Mr. Donald Shepard, of the Kennedy School of Government of Harvard University, who has reviewed the whole book with me, and given me invaluable advice on points of theoretical economics.

I should also like to thank Eileen Homer, Sally Ker, Wanda Boerke and Wendy Bennett for their help in typing, and the librarians of the Public Library of Concord, Mass., and of the Royal Institute of International Affairs in London and the Canadian Institute of International Affairs in Toronto for their kindly assistance.

In many of the matters discussed in this book, events are moving fast, and thousands of new facts and statistics are appearing all the time. The book will inevitably be out of date in certain respects on the day of publication. Nevertheless, the essential problems—national, regional, and global—with which it is concerned are likely to persist in their present form for at least the next decade.

To those people in the huts and villages of half the globe struggling to break the bonds of mass misery, we pledge our best efforts to help them help themselves, for whatever period is required—not because the Communists may be doing it, not because we seek their votes, but because it is right. If a free society cannot help the many who are poor, it cannot save the few who are rich.

PRESIDENT JOHN F. KENNEDY
Inaugural Address
January 20, 1961

one

THE GULF BETWEEN THE RICH AND THE POOR COUNTRIES

Since World War II the world has been divided, politically, into three major groupings. The so-called free world of Western nations (the countries of North America and Australasia, and most of those of Western Europe) have confronted the Communist bloc (the Soviet Union, the Communist countries of Eastern Europe, China, North Korea, North Vietnam, Outer Mongolia and Cuba) in the "cold war." The great majority of the remaining countries of the world, in Latin America, Africa and Asia, have chosen to remain "nonaligned" with either side, and so are loosely referred to as "the Third World." But under the surface of the cold war a new grouping has been emerging, based not on political systems and ideologies, but on the hard facts of wealth and poverty—facts which an illiterate peasant to whom such words as "Marxism" mean nothing, can fully comprehend. In this new alignment the world is divided into two major groups, the rich and the poor countries. The rich consist of the countries of the First World, together with the Soviet Union, the Eastern European countries and Japan, and the poor of all the rest. (South Africa, Rhodesia, Israel and certain small "poor" countries in Europe are special cases which fall outside the scope of this book.) Of the world's population of 3.8 billion (in 1972), 1 billion live in the rich countries and 4 billion in 1975 live in the poor countries.[1]

Per capita GNP (Gross National Product) figures provide a rough indication of the magnitude of the gulf between the rich and the poor countries. (GNP may be defined as the value of all final goods and services in constant prices.) The majority of the rich countries had, in 1975, a per capita GNP of around $2,000. The United States, with over $5,000, topped the scale. The majority of the poor countries had a per capita GNP of $200 or less. (The figures for China and

India, with a combined population of 1.4 billion, were $210 and $120 respectively.) Certain poor countries are reaching an intermediate stage; for example, the per capita GNP of Argentina is over $1,000 and of Libya nearly $2,000[2] (see Appendix). But they possess exceptional assets—Argentina a temperate climate and vast agricultural resources, and Libya new oil wealth. Essentially, however, the gulf is stark. The average citizen of a rich country eats a diet fully adequate for bodily needs. He lives a relatively healthy life for an average span of seventy years. He has free education in childhood and youth, easy access to health services, fresh water and electricity in his home and the use of modern means of communication. His living conditions are based on the technology of modern civilization. The average citizen of a poor country suffers from malnutrition, and lives in a relatively poor state of health for forty to sixty years. He is either illiterate or has a bare smattering of education, and his home is a hovel without fresh water or electricity, from which he seldom travels far. His living conditions are more like those of medieval peasants than of ordinary people in the rich countries: they have barely been touched by the transforming hand of modern technology. Finally, almost all the inhabitants of the rich countries, except for those of Japan, are "white," while almost all of the inhabitants of the poor countries are "colored." Racial emotions may therefore enflame the bitterness of the poor.

The poor countries are determined to "develop," to take their place with the rich countries in the emerging world community. As we shall see, they are making immense efforts and some progress—with a little help from the rich countries. But despite the efforts, the progress and the help received, the gulf between the two groups is widening. While their overall growth rates are broadly comparable, the fact that the population of the poor countries is growing at twice the rate of that of the rich countries means that the per capita growth rates of the former are lower. ("Growth" may be defined as the rate of increase of GNP.) Since growth is exponential, the gap increases. In 1970, for example, the United States' per capita GNP was forty-three times that of India; in 1980 it will, at present rates of GNP and population growth, be fifty-two times as great. The poor countries are officially called "the developing countries." But since the gulf is in fact widening, it seems more realistic simply to call them "poor."

The widening of the gulf is taking place in the context of the breaking down of the barriers which in all past ages have separated group from group and nation from nation. Modern ideas of science and the Rights of Man (see Chapter 3) and modern technology are creating the basis of a world society in which the "peoples of the United Nations," to quote the opening phrase of the United Nations Charter, share common interests and ideals. At the same time the realization is dawning that there just may not be enough resources of food, minerals and energy to support a world population which, at present rates of growth, will have doubled by the year 2000, at the standards of living set by the exponential growth of the rich countries. The pressures to close the gap between the rich and the poor, if necessary by controlling or even stabilizing overall world growth, certainly by massive sharing of resources, are therefore likely to become insistent within the next decade. U Thant put the matter starkly in 1969. "The members of the United Nations," he said, "have perhaps ten years left in which to subordinate their ancient quarrels and launch a global partnership to curb the arms race, to improve the human environment, to defuse the population explosion, and to supply the required momentum to development efforts. If such a global partnership is not forged within the next decade, then I very much fear that the problems I have mentioned will have reached such staggering proportions that they will be beyond our capacity to control."

We shall suggest in this book that the solutions to the problems of the rich and the poor countries lie in the development of "world community." What is a "community"? The modern mind is tormented by the dichotomy between freedom and unity. Freedom, it is felt, produces faction, while unity is equated with the dictatorial imposition of uniformity. But man is not merely a factious beast. All the great religious insights have asserted that when his spiritual nature is awakened, the free man spontaneously seeks unity, and that in this unity of brotherhood his freedom is enhanced. The force which unites free men is love. If we define a "community," therefore, as a form of social unity based on freedom, we must regard it as an essentially spiritual phenomenon, though most of the politicians, technocrats and social workers who are moulding the communities which we shall be discussing in this book—the European Community, the village communities in the poor countries, the potential World Community for the management of the oceans—might shy away from this thought!

Why are the rich countries rich and the poor countries poor? We suggest that the answer must be sought in the distinction between premodern societies (in the plural) and modern society (in the singular). The human race seems to be evolving from premodern forms of culture into a new or modern age; and for various historical reasons the rich countries are those which have entered the modern age first

—they are a mere two hundred years ahead. Our study must therefore start with a consideration of the basic features of these two kinds of society.

References

1. Population Reference Bureau, Inc., *1975 World Population Data Sheet* (Washington, D.C., 1975).

2. International Bank for Reconstruction and Development, *World Bank Atlas, Population, Per Capita Product and Growth Rates* (Washington, D.C., 1972).

two

PREMODERN SOCIETIES

Premodern man was an essentially religious being. He believed that through the faculties of the soul, that is, through imagination or vision or revelation, man could "know" the spiritual universe to which he intrinsically belonged, and he attributed to the soul his moral nature, his conscience, his sense of values and his power to act in accordance with these values. The rational and analytical faculties were used to *interpret* "revelation," not to analyze the "truth" of the revelation itself, or to see truth outside revelation. This attitude toward truth conditioned the political and social structures of premodern societies.

All the religions of the world, from the animism of the inhabitants of remote jungles and deserts to the metaphysical systems of the Orient and the monotheistic revelations of Judaism, Christianity and Islam, have affirmed not only that man is an immortal being, but also that the cosmos is peopled with other immortal beings, gods, angels, saints, jinn, fairies, goblins, witches, devils, and so on, with whom he is intimately connected, in this life and the next. Families and groups often claimed descent from a mythical god or hero, who became their presiding deity. Only in 1946, for example, did the Emperor of Japan formally renounce his claim to be descended from the Sun Goddess, Amaterasu. In many regions, particularly in Africa and the Far East, people communed regularly with the spirits of their ancestors, whom they felt to be directing their affairs. Since every human or natural event was thought to have a spiritual cause, it was thought also to have a spiritual remedy: the direct intervention of God, as in the experiences related in the Bible; the invocation of the protective power of the spirits or the saints; the conversion of bad into good karma by a life of moral rectitude; or resource to the magic of the witch doctor. What was *not* thought of was dealing with a natural event by natural means: the killing of mosquitoes with DDT, the preventing of smallpox by vaccination, or the increasing of crop yields by the use of fertilizers.

Since everything was spiritual, everything was sacred, holy, mysterious, marvellous or terrible. The modern distinction between the sacred and the secular did not exist. Life itself was a ritual. There was a right way and time to do things, in accordance with the cosmic order, and a wrong way and time, in violation of the cosmic order. These ways were revealed by visions, oracles, dreams, omens or astrological calculations. Everything in the cosmos was felt to be linked with everything else by a chain of psychic correspondences, a kind of spiritual gravity. Some things were "higher," others "lower," but all had their place and "degree" in the cosmos, and were innately in harmony. Man was an integral part of this order.[1] Evil consisted in the disturbance of this harmony by the sin or ignorance of humans or spirits. This outlook gave premodern man a deep sense of psychological security, which helped him to bear his physical insecurity and his material misery—though it also inculcated psychological fears of the consequences of violating this order.

Such an all-pervasive outlook produced a sense of group consciousness amounting sometimes almost to a collective identity. In social life, everyone *belonged*. The bonds uniting the members of the family—which was normally the "extended family" including grandparents, uncles, aunts and cousins, the "kith and kin"—the caste, the monastic "orders," the "orders" of knighthood and nobility, were fundamental and sacred, hallowed by the spirits, the gods or the saints. When a person committed a crime, all the members of the group were normally held responsible. If a person were sick or starving, the members of his group were morally bound to come to his aid. The concept of the responsibility of the individual *as such* did not normally exist.

Within the group each individual had a function which he or she was regarded as having been born to fulfil: being a priest, a warrior, a hunter, a merchant, a craftsman, a housewife, a tiller of the soil, a sweeper of the streets. Education consisted in training a boy or girl to fulfil his function; and often these prerogatives and skills were passed on from father to son for generations. The modern idea that every child should be educated to be himself, a unique, unpredictable person, that education should aim at drawing out his innate talents, whatever they might be, and preparing him to exercise these talents in his life, regardless of his position in the social group—this was generally unthought of.

Whether the basic political unit was a small village or a mighty empire, the underlying principle of government was the same: that the rulers were the representatives of the gods, or of God, the channel through which the divine power entered the body politic; they were godlike, semidivine; and if they failed to play their part, if they misruled and angered the gods, they could, in theory, be deposed. Political power was a sacred trust.

Rule by religious customs, interpreted by the priests and elders, produced an immense social stability. Everyone knew exactly how to behave in almost all the contingencies of life. The "agonizing decisions" involving personal judgment and responsibility, which confront most modern men daily, were reduced to a minimum.

The same communal attitudes governed traditional economic life. The inhabitants of the village normally owned the land in common and allotted it to families according to immemorial practices hallowed by religion. When they sought improved yields, they performed fertility rites. Some traditional societies had not, by the nineteenth century, invented wheels or ploughs. Except in times of disaster, a community normally was economically self-sufficient.

In those cultures which developed writing, scriptures appeared, and the function of the priest gradually changed from that of the magician who invoked the power of the spirits through ritual, to that of the scholar-lawyer who interpreted the teachings of the scriptures and formulated from them codes of moral and social behavior. The leaders of these cultures welded the scattered communities into great empires; written scriptures helped to foster uniformity of language and religion.

Large empires required organization. A ruling aristocracy often developed, sometimes based on the priesthood. Its members collected taxes, administered justice, kept order and led troops for the monarch. In return they were given land, so that an elitist economic structure of landlords and peasants emerged, the latter becoming, as time went on, increasingly tied to their landlords' land as unfree serfs, or tenants or wage-labourers. In cultures which had developed writing, the growing political and economic gulf between the ruling class and the mass of the people was enhanced by the fact that the former could read and write and the latter could not—it not being appropriate to their station in life. In these societies the written codes prescribing moral and social behaviour were even more rigid than the unwritten customs, because there was no longer the possibility of modification through direct appeal to the gods. This rigidity was particularly marked in China, in Hindu India and in Muslim societies. "No voices were heard unless they came from the tomb," said one British official of the Hindu and Muslim codes which the British found in force when they conquered India.

Many of these societies developed "culture" of the highest order: art, literature, philosophy, mathematics, architecture. The ancient Greeks thought out a number of abstract scientific hypotheses and applied science developed to a limited extent, for example, in the construction of pyramids, bridges and irrigation systems. The Chinese and Japanese invented printing in the early centuries of the Christian era. But the leap forward into modern technology was never taken.

When the modern age dawned in the nineteenth century, therefore, in all parts of the world, except for the white man in North America and Australasia, ninety percent or more of the common people were "peasants." All their lives, normally, they lived in the same village in which their ancestors had lived for centuries. They were illiterate, they were often hungry, they were the victims of famine, epidemics, and constant wars; and their normal expectation of life was twenty or thirty years. Public religion taught them that to try to change their lot was not only treason but heresy. As in heaven, so on earth. If human society were evil, and failed to reflect the cosmic order, this must be put right by "redemption" in another life, or by a return to the ideals of a Golden Age in the past, or by some spiritual apocalypse in the future. When at last men began to think of change, progress, development and "growth" as good *in themselves,* when they began to talk about the evolution of society *on earth,* then the modern age had dawned.

The premodern societies, grounded on religion, thus fostered in man an imaginative sense of belonging to a spiritual as well as to a physical universe, a sense of creative community with Nature, with other men and with God. But the price paid was the failure to develop the self-expression of the individual personality and its tool, the analytical reason: the enshrining of tradition and authority into social structures and the discouragement of the very idea of change. These factors inspired such seminal modern thinkers as Marx and Freud to reject the validity of all religious experience, Marx calling religion "the opiate of the masses," and Freud conceiving that it represented an immature psychological dependence on the image of an authoritarian father figure. Yet, as we shall see, modern man is now in urgent need of insights about the qualitative goals for his dynamic society (in the singular), which is grounded on the quantitative achievements of science. He is seeking for a new formulation of values in a secular culture; and he needs some power to inspire his will to express these values and to achieve these goals in a world which science can transform or destroy. When the great religions of the premodern age have shed the dogmatism, fanaticism and hypocrisy which Marx and Freud so rightly condemned, they may prove to be the essential complement to science in moulding the world community of the future.

References

1. For a discussion of this subject, see, for example, E. M. W. Tillyard, *The Elizabethan World Picture* (London: Chatto and Windus, 1960).

three

THE NATURE OF
MODERN SOCIETY

The distinctive feature of modern society (in the singular), in contrast to premodern societies (in the plural) is, we would suggest, that it is grounded on the principles of humanism and of science.

In its application to political, economic and social affairs, humanism may be defined as the attitude that *people, as such,* matter, that every individual has a natural or moral right to be provided, by society, with the opportunity to develop his or her creative potentialities. These Rights of Man have been written into most modern constitutions, including (with some limitations) those of the Communist countries, and affirmed in the United Nations Declaration of Human Rights of 1948. They may be divided into four categories: civil rights, such as freedom of worship, speech, writing, association and travel, and the right to a fair trial and the prohibition of torture; economic rights, such as the freedom to own and trade in property, to form trade unions, to strike, and to the free choice of employment; the political right "to take part in the government of [one's] country" [1]; and social rights, including the right to education, to work, to "just and favorable remuneration," [2] to rest and leisure, and to food, clothing, housing and care in sickness and old age.[3] These are, according to the United Nations Declaration, "the economic, social and cultural rights indispensable for [a person's] dignity and the free development of his personality." [4] A society grounded on these rights would be an ideal society—a "community." To establish such a society on earth is perhaps the deepest aim in the heart of modern man. He no longer looks *backwards* to a Golden Age in the past, nor believes that, because of man's inherent sinfulness, the ideal society can only come about in heaven.

The ideas of the modern age, which had been rumbling in the

Western European psyche since the Renaissance (though sparked off a thousand years earlier by the ancient Greeks), came into full flood in the countries of Western Europe and North America in the nineteenth century. Since the imperative need was to liberate the individual from overidentification with the traditional social groups—family, church, guild, caste, and so on—which had inhibited his creative self-expression, the emphasis at this time was necessarily on the first three kinds of rights. In particular, the right to the absolute personal possession of property, in contrast to the traditional concept of property as a social trust, was felt, especially in North America, to be necessary for this liberation. Except for the right to education, regarded as an essential adjunct to democracy, the social rights have been added mainly in the twentieth century. Are social rights compatible with economic and even with political and personal freedom? This has proved to be a major modern challenge.

The development of applied science in the first and second industrial revolutions has transformed man's physical life on the planet. Before the first industrial revolution all power, for all purposes, was generated by the muscles of men and animals, or by the movement of wind or water. The first industrial revolution, which dawned in eighteenth-century Britain, was based on power generated by machines operated by men—in the main by hordes of many unskilled "hands." The second industrial revolution, which started in the middle of the twentieth century, has replaced the unskilled hands by automatic machines, supervised by small numbers of skilled technicians.

The first industrial revolution led to urbanization, to the transformation of agriculture from a way of life into an industry, and to the transport revolution, making possible the speedy movement of men and goods, so that the great industries could be fed with raw materials drawn from all parts of the world.

These three great technological revolutions have transformed man's material environment. They have made it possible to implement social rights, to give all the citizens of industrialized states the material basis for the full expression of their humanity, while a fourth revolution, that of medicine, has lengthened the life span to two or three times that of the average person in past ages.

Capital—accumulated investment in building and equipment—is a basic prerequisite for industrial development. In Western Europe and North America the first crucial phase of industrial development, laying the infrastructure of the modern state—the building of roads and railways, the opening up of mines, the manufacture of steel and of machine tools, the generation of electricity, and so on—occurred in the nineteenth century, when the prevailing economic philosophy was that of laissez faire. Economists and politicians believed that government regulation of the economy was not necessary, because the "laws" of supply and demand would automatically allocate goods and resources effectively. They were not concerned with social justice. They believed, rather, in "Social Darwinism"—the survival of the fittest in the economic struggle.

By the beginning of the twentieth century the economies of the countries of Western Europe, North America and Japan were industrialized, and "growing"—the average rate of growth in the United States being 4 percent. One major result was that technology allied with the Rights of Man to undermine the organic groups of the premodern world in which each person fulfilled his part for the good of the whole and the glory of God. But the free and equal citizens did not prove to be fraternal. Man exploited man for private profit. The feudal caste structure was thus replaced by the modern class structure consisting of "bourgeoisie" and "proletariat," "management" and "labor," not bound together by the Church, as were the nobles and peasants of olden days, but separated by deep divergencies of attitude and interest. A second result was the instability of the laissez faire economic system, its succession of frequent booms and slumps, producing spells of grave unemployment. The worst was reached in the Great Depression of 1929–33, when world trade fell by twenty-five percent, and industrial production, in the United States, by forty-six percent, while unemployment soared to nearly twenty-five percent of the labor force in the United States and Britain, and thirty percent in Germany. Before World War II it was generally thought that these booms and slumps were an unavoidable phenomenon in the economic system.

The industrial revolution made the majority of the industrialized countries increasingly dependent on imports. Britain, for instance, has to import almost all its industrial raw materials except coal and iron, and half its food; while Japan has to import all its industrial raw materials. The United States and the Soviet Union have hitherto been largely self-sufficient; but in the seventies even they are beginning to import certain vital commodities—the United States some oil and key minerals, the Soviet Union, wheat. Thus an international economy has been steadily developing since the middle of the nineteenth century. Because of this, booms and slumps are international phenomena. But the reaction is often nationalistic: to insulate one's state from another's unemployment or inflation by trying to be economically self-contained and increasing tariff "protection," and thus producing a contraction of the world trade vital to the well-being of many states.

The Great Depression was exacerbated by high tariffs which had started to choke off trade in the late twenties.

The negative aspects of industrialization in Western Europe and North America—the social horrors of life in the "dark satanic mills" and their adjacent slums, where the hands who made the capitalists' profits toiled and dwelt; the social sufferings caused by the booms and slumps—produced a reaction against the philosophy of laissez faire. Three kinds of positive policies have emerged to replace or modify private-enterprise capitalism: those of socialism, economic planning and the welfare state, based on the social Rights of Man.

Socialism asserts (to put it crudely) that if the capital needed for economic development were in public rather than in private hands, then the society's income could be more justly distributed. The British Labour Party's constitution of 1918 defined the objectives of socialism as: "To secure for the producers by hand and by brain the full fruits of their industry . . . upon the basis of the common ownership of the means of production and the best obtainable system of popular administration and control of each industry and service." In practice, socialism has developed into national government ownership, or "state capitalism," although ownership is also often vested in lesser public bodies such as municipalities, county councils, or, in Communist countries, collective farms.

Karl Marx turned socialism into a philosophy of history, amounting to a secular religion. He asserted that public ownership was not only morally right, but inevitable. Human history would be consummated in communism; world-wide socialism would reach a point when the "state," as an administrative organization involving coercion, would "wither away," and all men, owning all capital assets in common, would spontaneously organize themselves fraternally.

Socialist philosophy has had a strong internationalist complexion: it has asserted that the real divisions in the world are not the political divisions between nation and nation, but the economic and social divisions between the "workers" and their exploiters, the capitalists. (In practice, however, the workers have often proved as chauvinistic as their exploiters.) After the establishment of the first Marxist state in the world in Russia in 1917, the world socialist movement split, broadly, into two major groups. On the one hand are "Socialist" parties, non-Marxist, or semi-Marxist, pragmatic and democratic, of which the British Labour Party is the prototype. (Some Socialist parties, such as the powerful German Social Democratic Party, did not shed theoretical allegiance to Marxism until after World War II). On the other hand are the Marxist Communist parties. The Socialist parties believe that the political system of democracy is more important than the economic system of public ownership; and so they have been willing to operate within a constitutional system allowing freedom to political parties which do not believe in public ownership. This attitude reflects their economic pragmatism. They have increasingly worked for a mixed economy, in which the basic public utilities such as railways, electricity, gas, waterworks, coal mines, banks and certain major industries are owned and operated by the state—the expropriated private owners being compensated, not liquidated, as they were in the Soviet Union. This "public sector" is complemented by a "private sector," consisting of a large number of enterprises which are regarded as more appropriately developed through private ownership and profit. Finally, Socialist parties are normally prepared to work for international economic development and social justice through the framework of the existing nation states, and by peaceful means.

The Communist parties of the world assert that they are working for the creation of the new kind of world society revealed by Karl Marx. They have hitherto proclaimed, and in Communist countries practiced, the doctrine of the one-party state. Dictatorial power is vested in the Communist Party, the "vanguard of the proletariat," because *all* capital assets are state-owned and any party which stands for private enterprise cannot, therefore, be tolerated. They believe that the world Communist movement should be in the vanguard of history, helping to create the world Communist society—though the call to world revolution has been muted since Stalin's death in 1953.

Before World War II, Socialist parties were in power only in Scandinavia and, for very short periods, in Britain and France. Since 1945 they have been either in power, or highly influential, throughout Western Europe, putting a mixed economy into practice in countries which are already industrialized.

Russia was essentially an underdeveloped country when the Communist Revolution occurred. In 1931 Stalin said to a conference of Soviet industrial managers: "The history of old Russia is one unbroken record of the beatings she suffered for falling behind for her backwardness. . . . We are 50 or 100 years behind the advanced countries. We must make good this discrepancy in 10 years—or they will crush us." So he proceeded to knout Russia into modernization: to establish the industrial infrastructure of a modern society on the basis of state capitalism, through the harsh dictatorship of the Communist Party. (The Soviet Union has so far shown no signs of moving from what Communists call "socialism," that is, a society based on state capitalism enforced by all the powerful sanctions available to a modern state, to "communism," or the "withering away of the state" prophesied by Marx.)

The complete nationalization in the Soviet Union of the means of production, distribution and exchange enabled Stalin to initiate another great innovation, at this time not thought of in the private-enterprise countries, the idea of organizing the state-owned economy on the basis of development plans, which assessed production needs and laid down targets and priorities for several years ahead. Through the combination of state capitalism and planning the Soviet Union was able to make the transition from a premodern to a modern society in two rather than in five or ten decades, despite the terrible destruction wrought by the Germans in World War II, and also to avoid booms and slumps—the Soviet Union was unaffected by the Great Depression, partly because it had little to do with the outside world. But a heavy price has been paid: the personal and political as well as the economic Rights of Man have been largely withheld from the Russian people. Since 1945 the Communist countries of Eastern Europe have modernized on the Soviet model, with some variations, in particular in Yugoslavia.

During World War II the countries of Western Europe, whether belligerent, occupied or neutral, were obliged to establish government control over all sectors of the economy and to plan the use of resources strictly. Since 1945 most of them have adopted the concept of economic planning in the context of their mixed economies. Their planning is not arbitrary and imposed, as in the Soviet Union, but "indicative"—"guidelines" democratically worked out between representatives of democratically elected governments, employers and workers, the latter freely organized into trade unions. In the early seventies the United States is the only major non-Communist country which has barely begun to develop a mixed economy and long-term planning. The Communist countries of Europe, at the other extreme of the spectrum, have begun to realize the need to make their planning more flexible, as their industrialization becomes more sophisticated, and are therefore experimenting with a "socialist market economy," which allows some free play for supply and demand within the framework of state capitalism.

While the planners of the free-enterprise countries have been drawing up their medium and long-term forecasts, new ideas have developed in these countries about how to "manage" the immediate economic situation through government spending, taxation and credit policies. The economy can be slowed down when "overheated," and stimulated when sluggish, in order to control inflation and secure full employment. The general adoption of ideas of management—in the United States as well as in Western Europe—together with long-term indicative planning, is spelling the end of the laissez faire philosophy. It is becoming generally accepted that nation-states should deliberately steer their economies towards growth and a high level of employment. Concepts such as "models," "indicators," "systems analysis," "social engineering," "think tanks," are in the air. And the planners have as their tools millions of highly sophisticated statistics, organized for them by electronic brains which can do complex calculations in a matter of seconds.

Socialism and planning have been complemented by the development of the "welfare state," as the means of implementing the social Rights of Man. By 1939 a number of governments of the industrialized countries were providing pensions for the aged, widows and orphans, and minimum relief for the unemployed, and were helping to finance health and unemployment insurance schemes, to which employers and workers contributed, and the provision of working-class housing. But the system was patchy, leaving many contingencies uncovered; and the insurance schemes applied only to wage-earners, others paying private fees for separate and better services.

The Soviet Union initiated, in the twenties, a different kind of system of social security in which the state provides full coverage for all social welfare services. (In practice, these services were not fully established until the sixties.) After 1945 the "umbrella welfare state," which offers equal benefits to all citizens and for virtually all contingencies, began to be established in Western Europe. The fact that these benefits are financed mainly out of taxation means that wealth is being redistributed. In the United States the separate schemes for old age pensions and unemployment insurance established in the thirties, and the medical care established for the old and the poor in the sixties, have not yet been extended into an umbrella system. The creation of the welfare state also implies the principle of minimum incomes, which have been widely established through laws creating minimum wages or through systems of collective bargaining between trade unions and employers—whether government or private.

As a result of these major departures from the laissez faire philosophy, a new kind of relationship is developing between management and labor. In the Communist countries the trade unions were from the first adjuncts of the government, denied the right to strike. Gradually they are becoming partners with the government, representing the workers' interests, rather than acting as stooges. In the free-enterprise countries the "two sides of industry" tended to bargain from the entrenched positions of their particular interests, often in a spirit of bitter class hatred, with the strike and the lock-out as residual weapons. Increasingly, they are meeting on a basis of equality, even of partnership, together with a third party, the government, to discuss their problems in the light of the state of the national economy as a whole. Meanwhile in both Communist and free-enterprise countries the idea of involving the workers in the process of management, pioneered in Yugoslavia and West Germany, is gaining ground. "Participation" became a key word in the later sixties.

Since 1945 economic interdependence between the industrialized countries has greatly increased. Over 90 percent of the technology employed in Sweden, for instance, is developed outside Sweden. Japan's economic miracle has been based largely on buying the fruits of other countries' research. Millions of people are pouring across national frontiers in search of jobs, business deals or pleasure. A monetary crisis in one country affects a score of others in a matter of hours.

The quarter of a century since 1945 has therefore witnessed the beginnings of real cooperation between the rich countries in economic and social affairs, carried out through a host of international bodies, as well as through continuous informal consultation between officials, banks, businessmen and so on. Economic nationalism has been eroded. Many of the tariff barriers have been removed—although quotas and other types of discrimination remain (see Chapter 12). Capital and labor have been allowed to cross frontiers more freely. Convertibility has been established between most currencies. National monetary crises have been "managed" by international action, often taken within a matter of hours; and the basis of an international currency has been laid in the establishment of the "special drawing rights" in the International Monetary Fund (see Chapter 16). The international economy is beginning to be "managed." International long-term indicative planning has been launched by the European Community; and in the Organization for Economic Cooperation and Development (OECD), the non-Communist rich countries have developed the tools—detailed surveys and statistics—for such planning.

The results of all these activities have been impressive. First, the economies of the rich countries have been steadily growing. Before 1939 neither economists nor governments were growth conscious. The term "growth" was hardly used. It was simply assumed that under the laissez faire system there would automatically be progress. By 1970 an industrialized country which did not grow at a rate of 3 to 4 percent a year was regarded as an economic problem child. In Communist and non-Communist Europe real wages rose by rates ranging from

50 to 100 percent between 1945 and 1967.[5] Second, there has been an unprecedented redistribution of wealth through the tax-financed institutions of the welfare state. In both Communist and non-Communist countries, the workers are becoming "bourgeois." Third, the terrible booms and slumps of the prewar decades have been mitigated, the recessions of the fifties and sixties being relatively minor phenomena. Fourth, full employment has been largely achieved, at least in Europe and Japan. Fifth, the development of worker participation within industry (where it exists—it is only just beginning) and trade union cooperation with management and governments in welfare and planning is creating a new atmosphere in industrial relations. "Industrial democracy" is complementing political democracy in the Western countries, and perhaps providing a lead-in to it in the Communist countries. "When men ceased to abandon themselves to the allegedly automatic workings of blind economic forces and began consciously to control their economic and social progress, a turning point in history had been reached." [6]

The United States, whose overall technological development and national GNP overshadow that of all the other rich countries—the per capita GNP of the other major rich countries ranges from two-thirds to less than half that of the United States[7]—is also the country where there is the least public ownership and economic planning, and where the umbrella welfare state is not yet developed. This may be a major reason why social problems and tensions are more acute in the United States than in the other non-Communist rich countries. By the early seventies growth in the United States was beginning to become cancerous, producing overconsumption, unacceptable pollution and serious depletion of natural resources (see Chapters 18 and 20). The United States thus provides other countries with a model of what their technological future could be like, and an example of the dangers of failing to introduce positive economic and social policies. The new phase of chronic unemployment and inflation which began in 1968, necessitating the imposition of comprehensive controls in both the United States and Britain, may be a symptom of the failure of the non-Communist rich countries to keep their economic and social policies in line with their technological development. A new policy breakthrough is required.

In the Communist rich countries there are also symptoms of growing social tensions, particularly among the young people. There are signs that the masses, now raised from near-serfdom into a bourgeois way of life, may not much longer accept passively the denial of personal and political freedom. The point has been reached where, in the

Western countries, freedom must be fully grounded in social justice; and in the Communist countries, social justice must be crowned with freedom. Otherwise, in both kinds of country, the tensions may erupt in chaotic violence.

There is also a negative and sinister aspect to international relations. International fears and tensions, which increasing economic cooperation has not dissipated, are expressed in a spiralling arms race. In the early seventies annual world military expenditure amounts to over two hundred billion dollars, of which the poor countries, excluding China, account for only 6 percent.[8] This expenditure is one and a half times what all governments are spending on education, two and a half times what they are spending on health, and thirty times more than the total of all governmental economic aid to the poor countries[9] (see Chapter 14). Military research and development absorbs the energies of a half of all the world's scientists and engineers, and costs some twenty-five billion dollars out of an estimated total expenditure on research and development of some sixty billion, only about 2 percent of which takes place in the poor countries, excluding China.[10] A report on the Economic and Social Consequences of the Arms Race, prepared for the Secretary-General of the United Nations in 1971, says: "The threat of ultimate disaster it [the arms race] has generated is by far the most dangerous single peril the world faces today—far more dangerous than poverty or disease . . . far more dangerous than either the population explosion or pollution—and it far outweighs whatever short-term advantage armaments may have achieved in providing peoples with a sense of national security. . . . The arms race makes more acute the very international strains to which it relates. . . . Armaments, which are supposed to provide security, provoke the very political differences which nations assume they will help to dissipate."[11]

The rich countries have started to create a new kind of society, based on the development of personal creativity through the implementation of the Rights of Man and the application of technology to the transformation of material conditions of living. They have opened up a marvellous hope to the poor countries—the possibility that the majority of people who today live in poverty and disease will one day be able to develop their human potential fully. Yet this hope is in danger of being shattered. We suggested in Chapter 2 that the influence of the traditional religions kept premodern societies in a static state. The dynamic modern societies have therefore necessarily rejected public religion, and become secular. But this has produced a schizophrenic split between their humanism—"people matter"—and their technology—"things matter." Modern man has not yet learned fully how to make machines the servants of his creativity. He has tended to become partially enslaved by them, by using them to minister to his greed and his destructive urges. In the early seventies it is beginning to look as if the crisis point of this schizophrenia is in sight: either the rich countries must leap forward into a new phase of psychological maturity, or begin to destroy themselves through overconsumption, pollution, domestic violence and, possibly, war. There is a growing affirmation, even at the official level, that the "quality of life" is as important as the quantity of things. A general revival of religious insights about the nature and destiny of man, in terms suited to the age of evolution, may provide the factor which could heal the split between heart and mind, and resolve the growing internal tensions in these countries. The eagerness with which millions of idealistic people have grasped at the utopian messianism of Marxism as a secular religion, and the failure of this religion to fulfil their hopes, may be a portent of the future; for the false gods precede the true ones. And here the poor countries, in which technology and secularization have not yet fully undermined ancient spiritual insights, have, perhaps, a vital role to play. It is significant that a growing number of young people in the Western rich countries are turning their backs on the material values of industrial society, trying to live simply and in tune with nature, and seeking inspiration in the insights of Hinduism, Buddhism and Islamic Sufism.

Such are the models which the rich countries offer the poor countries as they seek to enter the modern world. They are presented with a great opportunity: to modernize by adopting those features of the models which are both constructive in themselves and relevant to their own needs, while rejecting what is negative—for example, pollution, uncontrolled urbanization—and irrelevant. Most of the poor countries are trying to develop, as we shall see, on the basis of a mixed economy and economic planning. Only a few countries, among which India is outstanding, have managed to combine these policies with political democracy. The only major poor country which has succeeded in establishing a welfare state—China—has done so on the basis of complete socialism and the complete rejection of political democracy of the Western type. But in the face of their immense problems it would be premature to expect the poor countries to achieve solutions towards which the rich countries, with their hundred-year start, are only beginning to fumble.

Finally, we shall have to consider whether, as the world moves inexorably towards greater interconnection, the models of the mixed economy, economic planning and the welfare state, all grounded in democracy, are not becoming increasingly relevant on a global scale; whether they are not the models for a world community.[12]

References

1. United Nations Universal Declaration of Human Rights, Article 21.
2. *Ibid.*, Article 23.
3. *Ibid.*, Article 25.
4. *Ibid.*, Article 22.
5. International Labor Office, "Fifty Years of Social History: A Statistical Outline," in *Yearbook of Labor Statistics 1968.*
6. Statement of Mr. Archibald Evans of the International Labor Organization.
7. World Bank statistics, 1972.
8. United Nations, *Economic and Social Consequences of the Arms Race and of Military Expenditures: Report of the Secretary-General,* A/8469/Rev. 1, 1972, pp. 7 and 10.
9. *Ibid.,* p. 16.
10. Stockholm International Peace Institute, "The Nuclear Nightmare" in *The UNESCO Courier,* November 1975. (UNESCO, Paris.)
11. United Nations, *Economic and Social Consequences of the Arms Race, op. cit.,* p. 36.
12. For much of the material in this chapter, and some of the basic ideas, I am indebted to my friend Mr. Archibald Evans, formerly of the International Labor Office.

four

NATIONALISM AND INTERNATIONALISM

Politically, the world of the early seventies is divided into some hundred and forty sovereign nation-states, together with their dependencies. The "state" is essentially an administrative structure, an area of modern government, a framework for all the organizations of modern life—political parties, trade unions, welfare services, police and military forces and so on. A "nation," is a group of people who feel emotionally united by such factors as race, language, religion and a shared cultural heritage. The nation-state is "sovereign" because it has complete authority over its own affairs, owing allegiance to no superior power. In Europe, the state and the nation are, with small exceptions, coterminous; this fusion also applies to Japan, and is being rapidly achieved in North America. A citizen of a rich country has rights in, and duties to, institutions which have nothing to do with traditional groups based on birth and sanctified by religion. He can express his personality through voluntary membership in a vast range of public and private bodies, which flourish within the framework of the state. And he shares with his fellow citizens a revered national culture, expressed through a rich and living national language and literature. It is natural, therefore, that he should feel a deep emotional sense of nationalism.

In the poor countries, with the major exception of China, the situation is very different. Most of them owe their very existence to the predatory activities of the European colonial powers. The Spanish and Portuguese conquerors of Latin America imposed European government, religion and languages on Indian peoples who to this day have remained largely isolated, culturally, from the white man. When the Spanish colonists threw off the colonial yoke in the early nineteenth century, the continent disintegrated into twenty states based on the private kingdoms of the revolutionary leaders. But "Latin America is not a group of nations. It is one great disjointed nation," a leading Latin American has said.[1] Africa, the Arab world and, to a lesser extent, Southeast Asia were simply carved up into colonies by the European powers, without reference to geographic, ethnic, cultural or linguistic factors. Africa was "balkanized" into over thirty separate states, ranging from the huge Belgian Congo to the tiny Gambia. The Arab world, united by religion and culture, was artificially divided into thirteen states. An artificial unity was imposed on the Indian subcontinent and the Dutch East Indies. Each power ruled its colonies in its own way, establishing its own languages and institutions, developing industry and communications to suit itself. In West Africa, for instance, where French colonies were interspersed with British, the British and French built railway systems which did not connect with each other.

When independence came to the poor countries, the only organic social units within the largely artificial frontiers of the new states were often the—now disintegrating—traditional groups. Such "national" institutions as political parties and trade unions have tended to be tribal or caste units in modern dress. The citizen is torn between his ancient and sacred ties to these groups, and his realization that they must be broken down because they inhibit the development of the individual *as such,* and block progress towards the large-scale and impersonal administrative system which a developing economy requires. His problems of national identity and self-expression may be acutely enhanced by problems of language. In many areas, particularly those in which written scripts did not develop (that is, throughout Africa, and among the Indian peoples of Latin America and so-called primitive tribes of Asia) neighbouring villages speak mutually incomprehensible languages. All-India Radio broadcasts in fifty-one languages and eighty-two tribal dialects. In Mexico there are about ninety languages, and even the Sudan has a similar number. If he wishes to live as a citizen of his country rather than just as a member of his traditional group, a person living in such a country may have to learn the national language, which may be in effect a foreign language— Spanish in Latin America or Swahili in Tanzania or Hindi in India —or even the language of a completely alien culture, such as English or French.

Most of the poor countries are, at present, as fervently nationalistic as the rich countries. Their existing frontiers, however arbitrary and unviable, contain, as the legacy of colonialism, a state system which is in some measure a going concern. The immediate preoccupation of the new leaders is, naturally, to master this system; and a somewhat artificial fostering of nationalism may seem necessary to mobilize popular support and to prevent disintegration into separate "nations"— which has threatened Nigeria, Zaire, India, the Sudan and other states. The need of some hitherto remote and obscure people—the Yemenis, the Maldivians, the Fijis—to establish their identity in the world arena of nation states may inspire attitudes of nationalist self-assertion. The nationalism of the poor countries may, nevertheless, prove to be a short-term phenomenon. The circumstances of history have given their citizens a unique opportunity, denied to most citizens of the rich and well-established nation states, to blend the premodern and the modern cultures within their psyches, and thus to develop a cosmopolitan or global consciousness. From the end of the eighteenth century the Rights of Man were being asserted as a moral code on which government and law within states should be based. This has meant replacing government by traditional religious custom or by the arbitrary will of monarchs claiming to rule by divine right, with constitutional government by secular laws. These laws are normally related to the practical needs of changing situations, so there is no implication of heresy or treason in proposing their alteration. And constitutions and the personal rights enshrined in them have to be enforced, through legal systems, police forces and systems of "correction."

Although constitutional government is a secular activity, profound moral issues are involved. "Law" is not the same thing as "justice." From the time of Socrates philosophers have argued about what justice is and how laws can be brought to conform to it. Suffice it to say that the Rights of Man represent the nearest that modern man has come to formulating a public code of justice. Thus the modern sovereign nation-state, whatever its official ideology, normally establishes some form of constitutional government, implying that secular laws should subserve the ideals of justice.

For some three hundred years after the collapse, in the sixteenth century, of the Roman Catholic Church's moral authority over the rulers of Christendom, relations between the sovereign states of the Western world were conducted in terms of amoral power politics, "international law" providing the rules of the game. In 1919 President Wilson of the United States launched the idea that the moral principles of the Rights of Man should be internationalized. His initiative led to the establishment of the League of Nations, the International Court of Justice and the International Labor Organization. The United Nations, rising phoenixlike from the ashes of the League's demise, represents, together with its "family" of Specialized Agencies, a considerable expansion of this ideal. Its Charter enjoins it to maintain peace, stop aggression and promote economic and social development and the establishment of human rights. It is a kind of constitution for the world. Its membership, by September 1973, was almost universal. Only six states were not included (five for political reasons and one, Switzerland, of its own free will), together with a small number of territories still under colonial rule, the two groups containing a total population of some 120 million, out of a total world population of 3.8 billion. The United Nations is essentially an organization of sovereign nation-states; each of its members, big or small, rich or poor, powerful or weak, has one vote in its General Assembly (except for the Soviet Union, which has three). The hundred or so poor countries have a clear voting majority in the General Assembly, and their desire to retain this may be an important reason deterring them from federating.

The establishment of the United Nations ushered in an era of internationalism. Since 1945 the world has been carpeted with international bodies, regional, interregional and functional. These bodies have been occupied, for over twenty-five years, in making myriads of decisions in almost every field of human activity, in matters ranging from safety regulations for merchant ships to rules about the use of outer space, which many governments agree to put into practice in their domestic legislation. Thus a system of international customary law is developing, in a hand-to-mouth way, to complement the untidy pattern of international constitutional government operating through all the overlapping organizations. But one vital factor is lacking: real executive and enforcement powers. Only very small moves in this direction have been taken: the right of the United Nations Security Council to impose mandatory sanctions on a country whose actions threaten world peace—which has been done, not very successfully, in the case of Rhodesia; the raising of an ad hoc United Nations' army to stop the aggression of North Korea; the despatching of ad hoc United Nations peace-keeping forces to certain trouble spots; and the trials of the Nazi and Japanese leaders after World War II for committing the new "international crime" of waging aggressive war. In the crucial matter of disarmament, the United Nations, despite continuous efforts, has had no success at all. Certain international treaties have been made controlling the spread of nuclear weapons; and the United States and the Soviet Union have agreed to freeze the numbers of some of the items in their mighty arsenals. But the rich countries have not agreed to reduce any of these arsenals—basically, it seems, because they are not yet prepared to create a permanent peace-keeping force under international control. If a system of world constitutional government and world law is to emerge, at some point the leap forward will have to be taken into supranationalism, into a surrender of national sovereignty to bodies with real executive and enforcement powers. A prototype for supranationalism already exists in the European Community—an official, intergovernmental body called a "Community" is a new and unique political creature. It is inspired, not by a philosophy, but by an attitude, described by its founder, Jean Monnet, as follows: "Most people are well-intentioned, but they see only their own point of view. The thing is to bring them together round a table and make them talk about the same thing at the same time. . . . Work for common ends and means—create solidarity in practical matters, and ideas about class war, national rivalries and hereditary hatreds will disappear of themselves." After World War II the European federalists attempted unsuccessfully to create a federal constitutional structure for the United States of West Europe. Most of the nation-states concerned were not yet prepared to surrender sovereignty in such vital matters as foreign policy and defense. (The Council of Europe which was set up has powers only to make recommendations to governments.) The federalists then adopted a "sector" or functional approach, introducing creeping supranationalism into the supervision of the coal and steel industries of six countries. (The question of the ownership of these industries, whether public or private, was not affected.) When this proved successful, they extended the scope of the Community to all economic matters. The Community itself is still a constitutional hybrid, half international, half supranational; but it is in process of evolution and should logically move forward to become a full supranational structure. This would involve majority voting within the controlling Council of Ministers and the full accountability of its executive Commission, which already has wide powers of initiative and action, to the European Parliament; the direct election of this Parliament; and the extension of the Community's functions to political and defense matters. This functional and creeping approach provides a possible model for the development of a world community. Indeed, the community process, though very rudimentary, has already reached a point in the United Nations and its Agencies where, according to one authority, "there is really no way, short of world war, that [it] can be stopped or reversed. The process is rudimentary, because the world society in which it is taking place is rudimentary, and is only dimly aware of itself as a society." [2] One of the major prerequisites for expanding this awareness is that the poor countries should be brought into the modern world.

A crisis point seems to be approaching in international affairs. As U Thant has pointed out, the nations of the world are confronted with problems too dangerous to be left unsolved, too big and urgent to be solved by purely national or even international action. A leap forward into real world community may be in the logic of events. In the rest of this book we shall consider the problems of the poor countries in this context, and then finally discuss what forms the world community might take.

References

1. Felipe Herrera, "Economic Integration and Political Reintegration," in *Latin America: Evolution or Explosion,* ed. Mildred Adams. (New York: Dodd, Mead & Company, 1963), p. 95.

2. Donald F. Keys (Representative at the United Nations of the World Federalists), "The Seeds of Planetary Management," paper presented to the World Peace Seminar Conference, New York, April 8, 1972.

five

THE PROBLEM OF
POPULATION EXPLOSION

From some ten thousand years ago until the eighteenth century, the population of the world grew at an average rate of perhaps 0.1 percent a year. It is estimated to have reached 500 million by 1650. By 1830 it had doubled, to one billion. By 1930 it had doubled again, to 2 billion. By 1960 it had reached 3 billion, and by 1973 nearly 4 billion. At the current rate of increase of 2.0 percent a year, the world's population will be 7.5 billion by the end of the century.[1] In 1973 two-thirds of the world's population are living in the poor countries; by the end of the century the proportion will have risen to four-fifths. The number of years in which, at current rates of growth, the population of the various regions will double is:

Latin America: 25
Africa: 27
Asia: 30
North America: 63
Soviet Union: 77
Europe: 99[2]

Nearly all traditional societies extolled fertility. First, it was considered to be of profound spiritual importance to bear descendants. The lifeforce of the family's first ancestor, the god or hero, must be handed on. Second, children were an all-important labor force, helping their parents at work, and supporting them in old age. This support was not only a religious and moral obligation but a practical necessity when public health services and old age pensions did not exist. And since child mortality was very high, a large family was an essential insurance against spiritual extinction and loss of labour. Third, in some parts of the world, notably in Latin America, a man felt it necessary to have many children in order to demonstrate his virility—*machismo*. Fourth, many governments wished to expand population in order to increase their national power. Some of the leaders of the poor countries today, especially those in Africa, have denounced Western exhortations to practice birth control as a neo-imperialist plot to keep them weak and backward.

Traditional societies regarded conception, the quickening into life of a human soul, as a sacred operation. This attitude inspired the Roman Catholic Church's opposition to birth control, finally affirmed in the encyclical *Humanae Vitae* of July 25, 1968. The other major religions have taken a less dogmatic attitude, although some modern Muslim theologians are condemning birth control as a sin,[3] and Gandhi was strongly opposed to it. In general, until very recently, the subject of sex was surrounded by traditional taboos which inhibited objective and public discussion of population policies.

The population explosion started in the rich countries in the nine-teenth century. As late as the eighteenth century the average expecta-tion of life in Britain and New England was thirty or thirty-five years —it was perhaps twenty-five years in the Roman Empire. Most women spent the main years of their short adult lives in childbearing, and most of their children died in infancy or childhood. The medical, in-dustrial, agricultural and transport revolutions caused a dramatic re-duction in the death rate by controlling and curing diseases, and by providing better food and living conditions. By 1970 the average ex-pectation of life in the rich countries was about seventy years. The rate of population growth rose from about 0.2 percent in the early eighteenth century, to 1.0 percent in the nineteenth and twentieth centuries. After a time lag of some decades, however, the birth rates in these countries has begun to fall. The average woman is bearing two to four rather than ten to fifteen children. By 1972 the average popula-tion growth rate for the rich countries was 0.7 percent for Europe, 0.9 percent for the Soviet Union, 1.1 percent for North America and 1.2 percent for Japan.[4]

The basic cause of the fall in the birth rate of the rich countries undoubtedly lies in the very fact that they have become "developed." When a certain level of material affluence and psychological sophisti-cation is reached, the traditional reasons for wanting large families fall away. Children must be given material surroundings and educa-tional opportunities undreamed of in the past. The modern woman does not want to spend many years in childbearing and rearing, but desires an interesting life as a *person*. The scientific and humanist climate of thought has broken down the taboos and secularized the reproductive process. "Family planning," which in the past would have appeared sacrilegious, is accepted as sensible—like economic planning—and efficient methods of birth control have been developed to implement it.

In the mid-twentieth century this change of attitude produced a breakthrough in governmental policies. Negative policies of removing restrictions on the practice of birth control have been supplemented by positive policies of governmental promotion of family planning. In countries such as Britain and Sweden, where the welfare state is highly developed, family planning is regarded as an essential component of integrated health and welfare services for all citizens. In 1967 the United States Congress began to provide federal allocations for family planning and population research, to be carried out by voluntary and governmental agencies. And public discussion of birth control methods was launched for the first time in the Soviet Union in 1968 [5]—representing a major dogmatic volte-face, for Marxists have hitherto preached that overpopulation is a by-product of capitalism, which promotes surplus population in order to drive down wages. The greatest birth control success story of the rich countries is, however, that of Japan. In 1945 the country was laid low. Ninety percent of its productive capacity was destroyed, ten million people were unemployed, and it was stripped of the overseas territories which it had conquered to provide living space for its soaring population. The Japanese Government decided that birth control was essential to national recovery. Abortion was legalized in 1948, and in 1952 the government initiated nation-wide birth control education and the provision of free contraceptives. These measures, which brought the population growth rate down to 1 percent in the sixties, provided the indispensable basis for Japan's "economic miracle," which has made her, by the early seventies, the third industrial power in the world.[6]

These changes in attitudes and policies mean that families are now being planned, just as national economies are being planned, in the broader interests of parents and children. Parents are thinking of their future children as *persons,* who will lead significant lives in their own right, rather than as extensions of their ancestors and themselves.

Pope Paul VI, while condemning the *means* of family planning in his encyclical *Humanae Vitae,* affirms the *principle.* "Responsible parenthood," he said, may mean "a decision, made for grave motives and with due respect for the moral law, to avoid for the time being, or even for an indefinite time, a new birth."

At the beginning of the twentieth century the average expectation of life in the poor countries was about thirty-five years. The impact of the scientific revolution on the population situation in these countries occurred in the middle of this century, and in a far more sudden and explosive way than in the rich countries. In World War II the armed forces of the Western powers spread out around the world, bringing with them the means of "death control" which they were developing ever more rapidly for their own use. After the war decolonization stimulated the local desire for progress, and international bodies such as the World Health Organization continued the work which the armed forces had begun. Perhaps the two greatest postwar measures of death control have been the use of DDT to control insects and antibiotics to curb diseases, and the improvement of nutritional standards, especially the rising intakes of protein—though protein shortage remains the greatest single health menace in the poor countries (see Chapter 8). The leap forward in life expectancy has been dramatic. India, Mexico, Costa Rica, Venezuela, Ceylon, Singapore and Malaysia are among the countries which reduced their death rate by fifty percent between 1940 and 1960. By the early seventies the average expectation of life has nearly doubled, to about fifty years.

In the rich countries the lowering of the death rate took place over several decades, and during the time lag between the fall in the death rate and the fall in the birth rate the population explosion was largely concentrated in the expanding industrial towns. The agricultural revolution, which was taking place simultaneously, was substituting machines for the toil of peasants' hands. The wealth produced by the rapid industrialization financed the transformation of agricultural productivity and the import of cheap food, if necessary. Thus the exploding population was adequately fed, and the factory hands were able to produce the wealth for capital development.

In the poor countries, on the other hand, the leap forward in life expectancy has occurred in two decades, and the increase is spread equally over the countryside and the towns. Their population explosion has also been much bigger than that of the rich countries—an average rate of increase of over 2.5 percent, as compared with the wealthier nations' 1 percent. This and other factors which we shall discuss in the following Chapters make it very difficult for them to produce the capital required to finance improved agricultural productivity, food imports and industrial development. In the poor countries, therefore, the central factor which in the rich countries brought the birth rate into a new balance with the death rate—a rapidly rising standard of living—is not present. The main contributor to the fall in the death rate is, in fact, the decline in infant mortality, so that the net reproduction rate accelerates as the children who in the past would have died grow up and become parents, and as improved nutrition and public health services prolong the fertility period in women. The result is that over 45 percent of the population in the poor countries is under the age of fifteen, as compared with 25 percent in Europe and 29 percent in North America (in 1972). This adds a frightening dimension to the problem of providing education and work for all. The poor countries have half as many adults as the rich countries have to support each school-age child. It is impossible, moreover, for any family planning or birth control measures to affect the overall rate of population growth before the late eighties, when the children already born will reach reproductive age. It takes sixty to seventy years after the fertility rate has reached the replacement level of two children a family for population growth to cease.[7]

The United Nations has made global population projections for the year 2000, on the assumption that from about 1985 the combination of birth control and slowly rising standards of living will have begun to reduce the birth rate. They have worked out three figures, the "high, medium and low variants"—7.1, 6.5 and 6 billions respectively.[8] An extension of the high variant to the year 2050 would produce a world population of fourteen billion. Mr. Robert McNamara, President of the World Bank, suggested in 1970 that on the most hopeful assumptions world population might become stationary by the year 2120 at fifteen billion.[9] It is certain that the world cannot support a population of fourteen or fifteen billion, and probably not of five or seven billion, without major technological breakthroughs; and ecologists are now suggesting that any significant increase over the present figure of under four billion may drastically disrupt the ecosphere. (The problems of resources and ecology in relation to population will be further discussed later in this book.) It is therefore clear that population control in both rich and poor countries is perhaps the crucial key to future progress. "We have only delayed the food crisis for another 30 years," said Dr. Borlaug, the initiator of the "Green Revolution" (see Chapter 17), when he accepted the Nobel Peace Prize for 1970. "If the world population continues to grow at the present rate, we will destroy the species."

In the first two decades after 1945, the rich countries failed to take notice of the population crisis in the poor countries. The United Nations target for the First Development Decade—the sixties—of a 5 percent GNP growth in the poor countries, was set without taking into account the effect of population growth on economic development.

Demographic studies provide the basic statistics for population projections, which are essential for economic and social planning. The censuses of most of the rich countries are now regular, thorough and accurate. But in the poor countries the systematic study of demography was, until recently, hardly thought of, either by governments or by universities. Since 1945 the poor countries have been assisted by the United Nations in taking decennial censuses. "When China reported a census in 1953, the last large part of the world was removed from demographic darkness." [10] The United Nations laid down international classifications, and then, in the late sixties, produced the first global projections, to which we have referred. (At the time of writing, United Nations projections on the basis of national censuses of 1970 are not yet available.) National governments and private organizations began also to look at the problem from a global perspective.

The sudden dawning of a collective awareness of the full gravity of the situation brought about a breakthrough in international policies. Since 1966 the United Nations and its Specialized Agencies have openly urged the global adoption of family planning, and offered practical help to promote birth control in the poor countries. The World Bank began in 1968 to make loans in support of family planning programs, and in 1970 the United Nations Development Program (UNDP) was allotted fifteen million dollars for population projects. The United States and other governments began to offer help in family planning as part of their official aid. These policies received a further impetus when the United Nations came to assess the results of the First Development Decade. The poor countries achieved their target of a 5 percent growth of GNP; but because of their population growth, it turned out to be a net growth rate of only 2.5 percent—equivalent to two dollars a head a year! The targets for the Second Development Decade have therefore been related to population projections (see Chapter 15).

By 1971 thirty-five countries, containing over 70 percent of the population of the developing world, had officially adopted population planning policies. They included four of the most populous countries of the world—China, India, Pakistan and Indonesia—some twelve Roman Catholic countries and Egypt, the major country of the Muslim Middle East. The governments of a number of other countries were providing assistance to family planning organizations. But about half the poor countries still had no government population policies and were giving no governmental assistance to family planning. These included most African and Latin American countries.[11]

The implementation of these policies requires the development of satisfactory birth control techniques, the provision of health and welfare services to administer them and the persuasion of millions of poor and ignorant couples to abandon their traditional attitudes and avail themselves of these services.

Contraception research is only just starting. Modern science has not yet developed any wholly satisfactory means of birth control. At present the most acceptable and effective methods are the intrauterine device (IUD), the "pill," abortion and sterilization. The IUD and the pill are being mass-produced in some of the poor countries, and the United States Government provides consignments of the pill to almost any country to which it is giving aid and which asks for it.[12] The health and welfare services required to administer these techniques are, however, generally rudimentary. In Indonesia, for example, there were in 1969 some twenty-five million women of reproductive age, and less than one hundred trained gynecologists, of whom five were women. The problem of changing attitudes is even more intractible.

India is an example of a country which is making great efforts to control its population. Government family planning services were introduced in 1951, and under the Fourth Five-Year Plan for 1969–74, over four hundred million dollars is being spent on them. The target is to reduce the birth rate from forty to fifteen per thousand by the end of the eighties. (The average birth rate for the rich countries today is seventeen per thousand.) The country is placarded with posters portraying four round faces—two parents and two children. Ten thousand rural family planning centers have been established to service five hundred thousand villages. For the women, the government has mass-produced the IUD; to men who have had at least two children, it offers free sterilization, carried out in clinics in urban department stores, and by travelling doctors who establish one-day "sterilization camps" in the villages. In 1972 the Indian Government claimed that ten million men and women had been sterilized, and that 13 percent of the ninety-eight million couples of childbearing age had been "protected." [13]

In 1951 India's population of 361 million was increasing at the rate of 1 percent a year. In 1971 its population of 547 million was increasing at the rate of 2.6 million a year. By 1972 the population had reached an estimated 585 million, but the growth rate had dropped one decimal point to 2.5 percent. This is, perhaps, a symptom of future trends. After the rapid decline in the death rate in the last twenty years, the balancing decline in the birth rate may just be starting. It is significant that this decline is most evident in areas where the Green Revolution is bringing the beginnings of prosperity.

China is at present the only poor country which has managed to reduce its birth rate significantly—to an estimated growth rate of 1.7 percent. This achievement has taken place in the context of the launching of a dynamic economy, in which a vast nation's energies have been aroused and directed into constructive effort[14] (see Chapter 10).

We have seen that the rich countries began to reduce their birth rates *after* achieving a high standard of living. It was in the context of this high standard that people began, spontaneously, to practice family planning, and government assistance followed. The poor countries are trying, with the help and encouragement of the international community, to set about the task from the other end: to persuade people to adopt family planning in order to raise standards of living. United Nations projections for the year 2000 are based on the assumption that nine hundred million births will be averted by birth control, and only ten million as a result of rising prosperity. A tremendous experiment has been launched, whose outcome will be momentous for the planet. All one can say, at this stage, is that the solution to the problem of the population explosion is deeply bound up with the solution to the problems which we shall be discussing in the following chapters.

References

1. United Nations Association of the United States, *World Population* (New York, N.Y.: 1969), p. 10.

2. Population Reference Bureau, Inc., *1972 World Population Reference Sheet* (Washington, D.C.: 1972).

3. *The Observer Foreign Service News Service*, No. 25296, London: June 20, 1968.

4. *The New York Times*, December 5, 1972.

5. *The Times* (London), August 1, 1968.

6. *The Victor Bostrom Fund for the International Planned Parenthood Federation*, Report No. 10, Fall 1968, p. 7.

7. The Population Reference Bureau, Inc., Selection No. 40, July 1972.

8. Figures sent to the author by the Director of the Population Division of the United Nations on September 24, 1971. (N.B. Later figures have not yet been produced.)

9. Robert S. McNamara, *Address to the Governors of the World Bank*, Copenhagen, September 21, 1970. (Washington, D.C.: The International Bank), p. 13n.

10. *Census*, in *The Encyclopaedia Britannica*, 1966.

11. *Family Planning in Five Continents*, International Planned Parenthood Federation Booklet (London: July 1971).

12. Information given to the author by Dr. Alan Guttmacher, President, Planned Parenthood World Population, New York, N.Y.

13. Donald S. Connery, "India Defuses the Population Bomb," in *Vista, The Magazine of the United Nations Association*, November–December 1972, pp. 24–9.

14. Population Reference Bureau, Inc., *1972 World Population Reference Sheet, op. cit.*

six

SOCIAL PROBLEMS:
LAND TENURE, URBANIZATION,
UNEMPLOYMENT, ELITISM

The population explosion in the rich countries has been accompanied by two other basic social phenomena: the shift of population from the countryside to the towns and the transformation of the nature of work by the use of machines.

Before the industrial revolution probably no more than 5 or 10 percent of the world's population lived in cities. In 1970, in the larger rich countries of the West, the percentage of the population living in cities ranged from 88 in Australia and 84 in Japan to 75 in the United States and 70 in France.[1] The total urban population in all the rich countries was expected to double between 1960 and the year 2000.[2] The percentage of those who actually gained their living from the land was much lower in 1970 even than the percentage of those inhabiting the countryside: 7 in the United States, 20 in Western Europe generally and 3 in Britain.[3] While industrialization has hitherto meant a flight to the towns where the factories were arising, the ever-declining number of farmers have been able to produce enough food to feed the exploding urban population. Meanwhile, in both the factories and the fields, the second industrial revolution is replacing large numbers of the unskilled workers by small numbers of skilled technicians.

LAND TENURE

In the poor countries the majority of the population still live in the countryside and gain their living from tilling the land—50 percent in Latin America, 80 percent in Asia and over 80 percent in Africa. The cities are growing fast, but because of the exploding population, they do not need to suck people off the land to man the factories—although a flight from the land is occurring, as we shall see later. A basic social problem of the poor countries is, therefore, to establish systems of land ownership and social structures which will make it possible for the millions of peasants to live as citizens of the modern world, encourage and assist them to produce enough food for the towns, as well as for themselves, and discourage them from migrating from the land.

We saw in Chapter 2 that premodern societies regarded land as a trust, to be used by individuals for the benefit of the traditional group. "I conceive that land belongs to a vast family of which many are dead, few are living, and countless members are yet unborn." This statement by a Ghanian chief expressed the general outlook. The modern attitude is to regard land as personal property, over which the owner has absolute legal and moral rights. The premodern system will tend to be enshrined in custom, based on religious sanctions; the modern system in secular codes of law, enforced by secular means. In many premodern societies, especially those of Africa, land was normally owned communally. In others, such as those of medieval Europe, many parts of Asia, the Arab world and Latin America, communal ownership had been replaced by feudalism. The peasant masses became small-holders, tenants, landless labourers, serfs or slaves, under the social domination and political control of the great landowners. When, in the nineteenth century (in Latin America) and twentieth century (in Asia and the Middle East) modern systems of constitutional government were introduced and the illiterate peasants were given the vote, what else could they do, bribed or threatened as they often were, but vote for the person on whom they were so dependent? And the legislatures and governments, based on the landed interests, naturally opposed any idea of reforms which would break up their estates and divest them of power.

The most extreme form of feudalism developed in Latin America. At the time of Conquest, the Spaniards seized the Indians' lands, which were owned communally and cultivated with many crops which the Indians had domesticated. Most of the Indians became serfs (peons); the rest retreated to remote mountains and jungles. The system of great estates, sometimes called *latifundia,* has generally prevailed till the present day. Just over 100,000 landlords, or 1.5 percent of all the landowners, own 65 percent of all land in private hands. "Each of them owns an average of 4,300 hectares (10,750 acres); but many have more than 10,000 hectares and some have hundreds of thousands, even millions. . . . Properties belonging to several members of a family can be registered under the name of its head. There are Latin American families who own more land than is occupied by a number of sovereign nations. . . . This is a situation which has no parallel elsewhere," writes a Latin American sociologist.[4] Most of the holdings which are not *latifundia* are *minifundia*, tiny plots which are constantly being subdivided as a result of the exploding population. This land-tenure system has perpetuated a static and stagnant economy. By 1960 agricultural production throughout the continent had fallen about 10 percent below the pre-1939 levels. Most of the landlords are absentee, and many operate also as captains of industry. Their agricultural incomes are only a fraction of their total incomes. Their overseers are often ignorant of modern agriculture and management. They fear that modernization would arouse the peasants out of their habits of apathetic obedience. As a result of this system of land tenure, in 1968 about half the agricultural population of Latin America was, according to one writer, using methods of cultivation more primitive than those of ancient Egypt. They were without ploughs, oxen or wheeled vehicles. In Colombia, in 1960, 75 percent of all heads of household living off the land were relying exclusively on their own muscle power and that of their families.[5] On the other hand, where modernization has been introduced on the great estates, machines have replaced the labor of peasants' hands, or land has been switched from crops to grazing, which also employs fewer workers. Thus the basic pattern is that of either very primitive or highly modernized systems of agriculture, neither of which provide prosperity or opportunity for the peasant.

The Middle Eastern and Asian situations were broadly similar to that of Latin America, except that a higher proportion of the peasant population were tenants. This meant that the whole agrarian scene was darkened by the rapacious grip of the money lender. The Koran's prohibition of usury did not prevent millions of Muslim peasants from paying interest at exorbitant rates, not only to finance the rent in years of bad harvests, but also to cover the cost of dowries, weddings and funerals. In the Middle East the great estates were complemented, as in Latin America, by a high proportion of small plots; 94 percent of the Egyptian landowners owned less than five acres,[6] 70 percent of the rural population of China was landless.[7] In India much land was owned communally by the villagers before the coming of British rule. The British gave the tax farmers—*zamindars*—rights of private property over the land, and the *zamindars* gained control over the village communities, forcing the peasants into tenancy and the grip of the money lenders. These new rights of private ownership were supported by British law administered in the British courts.[8] Roughly the same situation developed in Indonesia under Dutch rule.[9] By the middle of the twentieth century the sufferings of the Asian and Arab peasant were greatly accentuated by the population explosion, for whereas Africa and Latin America are relatively underpopulated in relation to their size, there is little extra land to go around in the desert lands of the Middle East and the densely populated countries of Asia.

The following example from China may illustrate how the land-tenure system affected the Asian peasants.

"I grew up in the village of Fengchiatsah in Suiteh hsien [province]," said Ma Chen-hai, aged sixty-five, to the Swedish writer Jan Myrdal in 1962. "My family had always been farmers. We owned 15 mu and we rented 30 mu from Ma, the landlord. We had to pay 34 jin per mu in rent. . . . Ma had a money-lending concern. . . . We were not able to pay our rent. He took interest on it and interest on the interest . . . and in the end our debt increased to 1,200 jin of grain, so he took our 15 mu of land from us. . . . We could not get out of his clutches. . . . Father had no hope any longer. He did not dare talk with the others in the village. If he had, he would have been suspected of stirring up mischief. Mother just wept. . . . I gathered fuel and plucked grass. I looked after our goat and the landowner's donkey. . . . We never saw a government official and I have no idea when the dynasty went. At all events, we never noticed anything in our village of those revolutions. Everything stayed the same, and the farmers suffered just as much all the time." [10] *

In contrast to the situation in Latin America, Asia and the Middle East, Black Africa had, in general, no traditional land-owning class with vested interests, based on an exploited peasantry, which stood in the way of progress. The problem in Africa was to change, rather than to destroy, traditional social attitudes, so that new forms of land tenure could be evolved suited to the age of development.

In the words of Gunnar Myrdal, the Swedish economist: "In the pattern of agrarian reconstruction of developing areas, land reform is the focal point."

URBANIZATION

In the rich countries the industrial and agricultural take-off preceded the growth of the cities. In the poor countries, however, the growth of

* Reprinted by permission of Pantheon Books/A Division of Random House, Inc., and William Heinemann Ltd.

the cities is preceding agrarian and industrial transformation. Their growth rate is several times that of the overall population growth rate—for example, the population growth rate of Kenya is 3.3 percent a year, while that of Nairobi is 9 percent. It is estimated that by 1980 Shanghai will have a population of fourteen million, Mexico City of thirteen million, Sao Paulo and Buenos Aires of nearly twelve million, and Calcutta ten million.[11] The city population of the rich countries grew more slowly than the numbers of people working in industry; in the poor countries, however, the reverse is occurring.

The cities of the poor countries are therefore economically unhealthy phenomena. Many countries launched into development by embarking on ambitious programs of industrialization. "The idea behind this strategy was that the industrial sector would pull with it the backward agricultural sector and provide alternative employment opportunities to the rural population." But many of the new industries are not "labor-intensive." Often they are equipped with expensive, sophisticated labor-saving equipment which a rich country may have provided as "aid," or which the poor country may have bought with the idea of launching itself directly into the computer-nuclear age. In Brazil, for example, where there are very high rates of industrial investment, the number of industrial workers has been increasing by only 2.8 percent a year.[12] Algeria, bolstered by extensive French aid and new oil wealth, is channelling half of its five-billion-dollar four-year investment program into industrial development. "The major characteristic of the industries the Algerians want to establish is one [sic] of high efficiency and automation. The idea is to make them competitive in world markets." So "there will be no quick absorption of all the idle hands Algeria has at the moment." [13] Perhaps in the long run the highly efficient second industrial revolution equipment will be the best means of mass-producing the very large quantities of cheap consumer goods which the peasants need as incentives to increase agricultural production. But at present, because of the relative neglect of the agricultural sector, the peasants can afford only the most limited quantities of consumer goods, such as bicycles and cotton umbrellas, and many of the factories which produce them are working below capacity. Sometimes high tariff protection keeps these industries inefficient; or low production may be caused by bottlenecks and mistaken estimates in government planning. For example, the railway freight car plant at Bharatpur in India was obliged in 1971 to reduce its output to half capacity and to dismiss half its workers, partly because it lacked orders, but mainly because the government-owned steel plants were failing to supply the steel for the orders it had. Finally, high wage demands, minimum wage legislation, compulsory social insurance policies and so on make labor expensive, and thus add to unemployment. In Kenya an unskilled factory worker earns twenty-five cents an hour, an agricultural worker seven cents an hour. This unhealthy economic situation is reflected in the rapid growth of the service sector. In 1970, in Africa and Asia, the percentage of workers employed in agriculture was 67, in industry 12 and in the services 21. For Latin America the comparable figures were 34, 27 and 39.[14] In the rich countries the shift of labor from industry to services reflects increasing automation, a high level of consumer affluence and the growing desire to improve the "quality of life." The demand for shops, restaurants, gas stations, places of culture and amusement and so on is rapidly rising. But in the poor countries the high service sector means that millions who cannot get jobs in industry are eking out a miserable living as peddlars, shoe shiners, owners of small shops and stalls, or touts for the tourists from the rich countries. Many are supported by their relatives, or support themselves by crime.

In these cities expensive modern-style buildings which provide offices, shops and apartments for the new elite (see below) are shooting up everywhere, and so are the comfortable hotels for the mighty throng of tourists. But around the enclaves of the rich are a rash of vast shantytowns of shacks in which the indigent house themselves, often by illegal squatting—for the prices of land are very high, there is normally no mortgage system, and money lenders charge very high rates of interest, up to 100 percent. The population of the cities is doubling, roughly, every ten years; but the population of the shanty towns is doubling every five to seven years.[15] These settlements of misery normally lack electricity, clean water supplies, sanitation systems and paved roads. The worst areas of cities such as Calcutta, Hong Kong, Lima and Buenos Aires contain "the lowest standards of living and meanest quality of life ever known on this planet outside concentration camps."[16]

The urban explosion in the poor countries is a catalyst for social transformation. In the factory workshops and cafeterias, in the crowded buses and trains, in the schools and even in the pavement dormitories, the barriers of tribe, caste, sex and race are eroded. Even the unemployed shanty-dwellers are evolving their own subcultures, often with a strong sense of community, and sometimes of a semimilitary nature, as in Peru, where organized squatter "invasions" of land around Lima have occurred. But the breaking down of traditional social groups in cities whose authorities are failing to develop constructive policies for new ways of living is creating vacuums in which despair and vio-

lence breed. The population explosion is turning these great conglo-
merations of malnourished, semiliterate and unemployed people into
danger spots.

UNEMPLOYMENT

Massive unemployment and underemployment in the poor countries
was not anticipated in the early sixties. The strategy of the First Development Decade, launched in 1961 (see Chapter 15) was to concentrate on "growth," and to regard employment, in the words of
the ILO's World Employment Program, as a "byproduct of economic
development; it was assumed that unemployment and poverty would
disappear if only the rate of economic growth could be accelerated."
But "a number of developing countries experienced a very rapid rate
of growth of national income during the whole decade 1960–70 without any improvement (and sometimes a deterioration) in the employment situation." [17]

"In the developed countries, rapid growth has hitherto implied full
employment." [18] An unemployment rate of 3–4 percent in Britain is
considered barely acceptable, and one of 6 percent in the United
States is considered unacceptable. Yet the unemployment rate in most
poor countries ranges from 15 to 30 percent. A study produced by the
Organization for Economic Co-operation and Development (OECD)
in 1971 shows, for example, that "Uruguay has an unemployment
rate of 18.5 percent," that in Guyana "the unemployed comprise
almost half the population over 14; in Ceylon almost half the men
living in the towns are out of work. The study does not quote a single
underdeveloped country that has employment rates considered acceptable in Britain and other developed countries." [19] "A recent survey
indicated that in Kinshasa, in the Congo, a third of the men had no
jobs. In Lagos, Nigeria, no more than half the men are earning enough
to support themselves without help" [from their families].[20] In India
the urban unemployed are estimated at sixteen–seventeen million,
and if present trends continue they will be fifty million in 1979.
Rural unemployment in India is put by some officials at 30 percent.[21]

A basic cause of the employment crisis is that half the population
of the poor countries is under twenty; and that because of the lack
of educational facilities, a far higher proportion of those under twenty
are coming in to the labor market than in the rich countries. We
have already noted the relationship between land tenure systems and
rural unemployment. The peasant may either be underemployed in a

stagnant village community which offers little or no scope for self-improvement, or unemployed as a result of the mechanization of agriculture. Half the resident population of a thirty-seven thousand-acre estate in Ecuador was turned out when the farm was mechanized and made one of the most efficient in the country. In Brazil, employment on the biggest farms, accounting for 50 percent of the country's farmland, has declined by up to 50 percent in recent years.[22] Through film, radio, newspapers and travellers the unemployed peasant has heard of the big cities where new industries are shooting up. So he puts his old basket or suitcase on his head or his mule, and sets off for the unknown city several hundreds of miles away.

Two young men in a distant Senegalese town ask us for a lift to Dakar . . . two days' drive and a world away. They are shabbily dressed in clothes that are half African and half European, and they carry their belongings wrapped in a cloth. From their halting French, we guess that they attended primary school for a few years but did not graduate. [They are obviously going to stay with relatives and look for jobs.] We pass through a little village of thatched huts. The men were returning from the fields, and the women, dressed only with a wrap-around skirt, were gracefully carrying firewood on their heads long miles to their homes. . . . The peasants laughed and called greetings to us. To our surprise, one of the youths in the car burst out, with a bitterness rare in soft-spoken Africa: "Look at those people—they're savages—they don't know anything." It is from "those people," from tradition-bound peasant life, that those two young men are fleeing, because they have been to school for a few years.[23] *

The majority of the rural migrants arrive in the big city to find shantytown living conditions, no work and no unemployment relief or welfare services.

Such is the present position; and because of the population explosion, the rate of growth of the labor force is rising rapidly in the poor countries. According to the United Nations, in the seventies two hundred twenty-five million *more* people will be seeking jobs in these countries, and only fifty million more people in the rich countries.[24]

By the beginning of the seventies national governments and international organizations were recognizing that unemployment is one of the most critical problems in the poor countries. The International Labor Organization produced the first major overall survey of the problem in its *World Employment Program* of 1971. Population-control measures cannot immediately affect this situation, since all new entrants into the labor force of 1970–85 have already been born.

* © 1965 by David Hapgood. Reprinted by permission of Atheneum Publishers.

ELITISM

"The poorest quarter of the population in the developing lands risks being left almost entirely behind in the vast transformation of the modern technological society. The 'marginal' men, the wretched strugglers for survival on the fringes of farm and city, may already number more than half a billion. By 1980 they will surpass a billion, by 1990 two billion. Can we imagine any human order surviving with so gross a mass of misery piling up at its base?" asked Robert McNamara in 1970.[25] The misery of the masses of semiemployed and unemployed peasants and urban dwellers is thrown into sharp relief by the development of "elitism," a wide gulf of consciousness, class and standard of living *within* the poor countries.

In every society there has always been an elite, a group or class who wielded power and influence, and who were often trained for this purpose. In the premodern societies of the poor countries, and in the modern societies of the rich countries, the elite and the masses share the same culture. The Indian rajah in all his grandeur was linked to the peasants in their poverty by the all-embracing ethos of Hinduism. The way of life of an American Senator is merely a variation of that of his constituents. A major problem in the poor countries lies in the fact that if the local elites are to lead their peoples into the modern world, they must first enter this world themselves; they must develop a kind of consciousness which for a time will cut them off from the consciousness of the majority of their fellow countrymen. They must know, for example, how the international monetary system works, how to interpret statistics, how to organize epidemic-control campaigns. This very type of thinking is incomprehensible to the illiterate peasants, who for centuries have believed, as did their premodern elites, that natural and human phenomena are controlled by spiritual forces. Jawaharlal Nehru, Prime Minister of India from 1947–64, described the situation poignantly in his *Autobiography,* when he referred to himself as "a queer mixture of East and West, out of place everywhere, at home nowhere," experiencing a sense "of spiritual loneliness not only in public life but in life itself." The supreme challenge to the elites in the poor countries, therefore, is to *integrate* the modern consciousness into that of the traditional culture, to blend both worlds, rather than to reject one or the other. If they can achieve this, they may, as we suggested in chapters 2 and 3, succeed laying the basis for a new world consciousness. A small minority, in particular in India and Africa, have tried or are trying to do this. We shall discuss the political and social philosophies which they are working out in Chapter 11. But the majority have not been able rise to this challenge. Many are self-made men who have come to power through the army, often through violence or through the new constitutional channels (see Chapter 9). Their natural tendency is, like that of the Senegalese youths described above, to reject the values of their traditional societies and to emulate the material standards of the rich countries, inculcated by their Western-type education.

"In one primary school in West Africa," writes an American journalist, "I saw on the wall a poster (printed, naturally, in Europe), that set out the school's teachings with hideous clarity. The poster showed two family groups. One was seated around a table, eating from plates with knives and forks; this group wore European clothes and lived in a European-style house, shown in the background. The other family group was squatting around a large bowl from which rural Africans ate with their hands. The parents wore African clothes, the kids were naked, and they lived in a thatched hut, also shown in the background. More clearly than a thousand words, this tattered poster drove home the poisonous message of the school: one family group was good—modern, the other was bad—traditional. . . . After this devastating lesson it is not surprising that educated Africans often adopt the form of Europe without the substance—the consumption without the production, the table without the protein." [26]

The emotional insecurity of the new elite, their desire to "keep up with the Joneses" and to make their presence felt in the world of their former rulers—"the new nations are not content to emerge into only half the world," said the American diplomat, G. Mennen Williams—often expresses itself in an intense chauvinism. Personal status symbols are supplemented by national status symbols. Presidents and ministers of state wear immaculately tailored suits and ties (in contrast to the austere costumes of the top Chinese, Cuban and Indian leaders, which in the age of television have a great symbolic impact), live in palatial air-conditioned residences furnished with the latest glassware from France or Britain and drive around in Mercedes cars.[27] The palace of President Houphouet-Boigny of the Ivory Coast, a country whose per capita GNP is $260 a year, is said to have cost twenty million dollars; and for its construction, hundreds of tons of malachite were imported from Russia by air.[28] They pay themselves the same salaries and give themselves the same length of holidays as those of their former colonial masters, or of the expatriate whites whom they now employ. Motor cars are a preeminent status symbol. The mayor of Ouagadougou, the capital of Upper Volta (whose per capita GNP is $60 per year), has forbidden the use of small cars as taxis, while in order to counteract this elitism President Nyerere of Tanzania has ordered all government officials and ministers to use only small cars, and has forbidden the import of cars altogether unless the purchaser can prove government need—and a similar policy prevails in India. On the national level, television stations service a handful of viewers, sports stadiums and luxury hotels for tourists are erected, subsidized airlines are established and expensive embassies are sent abroad. Sometimes all this show is a cover-up for the incompetence and lack of savoir-faire of the army officers, former clerks and schoolmasters who run the government; and sometimes foreign aid, including Communist aid, panders to it. In Africa, perhaps, the trappings of elitism are at their most flamboyant and absurd. But the same phenomenon exists in the other continents. The gulf between the elite and the masses is accentuated by poor communications—it may be easier to travel to New York, London, Moscow or Peking than to one's constituency in the bush or the jungle—and by the problem of language—the elite often cannot communicate with the masses in their local tongues. When the Prime Minister of India visits the southern part of the country he or she is obliged to make speeches to huge audiences of uncomprehending peasants in English. A Senegaese official, visiting a remote village with an American, spoke in French to fifteen hundred people, and his speech had to be translated into four languages.

Thus at one end of the social scale is the rapidly growing mass of the primitive land-hungry peasants, the dwellers in the urban slums and the unemployed, the majority still living mentally in the pre-modern world; and at the other end are the elites, living mentally in the modern world, and at their worst, flaunting the vulger materialism of the West. To develop constructive policies for healing this gulf and establishing internal social integration is a major problem confronting the poor countries.

References

1. "The Problems Associated with Rapid Urban Growth," in *The OECD Observer* (Paris), No. 54, October 1971, Table, p. 6.

2. United Nations, *Growth of the World's Urban and Rural Population 1920–2000.* United Nations Population Studies No. 44 (New York: 1969), p. 75.

3. *International Labor Review*, Vol. 98, No. 4, October 1968, Table IV.

4. Oscar Delgarde, "Revolution, Reform and Conservatism," in *Latin America, Reform or Revolution?*, ed. James Patras and Maurice Seitlin (Greenwich, Conn.: Fawsett Publications, Inc., 1968), p. 383.

5. T. Lynn Smith, *Studies in Latin American Societies* (Garden City, N.Y.: Doubleday and Company, Inc., 1970), p. 235.

6. Tom Little, *Modern Egypt* (New York: Frederick A. Praeger, Inc., 1967), p. 221.

7. Keith Buchanan, *The Transformation of the Chinese Earth* (London: G. Bell and Sons, Ltd., 1970), p. 35.

8. Charlotte Waterlow, *India* (London: Ginn and Co., Ltd., 1969), pp. 47–48.

9. Leslie Palmier, *Indonesia* (New York: Walker and Co., 1966), pp. 68–69.

10. Jan Myrdal, *Report from a Chinese Village* (Middlesex, England: Penguin Books, Ltd., 1967), pp. 197–98.

11. United Nations, *Growth of the World's Urban and Rural Population, op. cit.*, p. 65n.

12. Erich H. Jacoby, "The Coming Backlash of Semi-Urbanization," in *Ceres, FAO Review*, Vol. 3, No. 6, November–December 1970, p. 50.

13. *The New York Times*, January 29, 1971.

14. International Labor Conference, *The World Employment Program* (Geneva: The International Labor Office, 1971), p. 11.

15. *Symposium on the Impact of Urbanization on Man's Environment: Statement and Conclusions*, held by the United Nations in cooperation with the United Auto Workers. (Washington, D.C.: UAW, 1970), p. 14.

16. *The Hungry Millions, A Textbook on World Development*, edited and published by the Workers Education Association (England) in conjunction with the Oxford Committee for Famine Relief (OXFAM), p. 39.

17. International Labor Conference, *World Employment Program, op. cit.*, p. 16.

18. Robert S. McNamara, *Address to the Board of Governors of the World Bank*, Copenhagen, 1970 (Washington, D.C.: World Bank pamphlet).

19. *The Weekly Guardian* (London), January 21, 1971.

20. *The New York Times*, April 30, 1971.

21. *Ibid.*, March 3, 1971.

22. Ernest Feder, "The Campesino is Still Waiting," in *Ceres, FAO Review*, Vol. 2, No. 6, November–December 1969, p. 27.

23. David Hapgood, *Africa from Independence to Tomorrow* (New York: Atheneum Publishers, Inc., 1965), pp. 9–10.

24. In an address at a conference held by the United Nations Association of the USA in Boston on May 27, 1971.

25. Robert S. McNamara, *op. cit.*

26. David Hapgood, *op. cit.*, pp. 160–61.

27. Partly based on discussion with Sir Edward Warner, formerly British Ambassador to the Cameroon and Tunisia.

28. René Dumont, *False Start in Africa* (London: Andre Deutsch, 1969), p. 80.

seven

THE PROBLEM OF EDUCATION

We pointed out in Chapter 3 that the development of free, public education was the only one of the social Rights of Man which the governments of the industrialized countries started seriously to implement before the twentieth century. In premodern times the great majority of the peasants were illiterate. They were *trained,* as their ancestors had always been, to perform the manual tasks related to their station in life. A small minority of scholars and gentlemen were *trained* to read and interpret the great scriptures of their culture, and to impart to a minority of the young *men* an education which consisted largely in memorizing these scriptures. Often these texts were written in a classical language—Arabic, Sanskrit, Pali, Latin—which had little connection with the everyday language of the scholar's or the student's life.

Literacy was thus allied to religion. The literate priestly and noble castes upheld the framework of spiritual concepts which provided all members of the society with a sense of divine purpose of life. Through the ages, however, the understanding of the deeper meaning of the scriptures tended to evaporate, and the traditional learning became pedantic. When the modern age dawned, the scholars were, for the most part, unable to relate this learning either to modern spiritual needs or to modern ideas of liberalism and science. The abolition by the Chinese Imperial Government in 1905 of the ancient system of examining civil service candidates in the three-thousand-year-old Confucian classics was a symbolic gesture as well as a practical reform.

Women were almost completely excluded from classical education, and except in those areas south of the Sahara and on the east coast of Africa which had been converted to Islam in the Middle Ages, Black

Africa had no writing, and therefore no elite of scholar priests and no scriptural education, before the coming of the Europeans.

The European colonists superimposed on this situation their own education systems. These in their turn were based on an uneasy marriage between premodern classical European learning, and modern ideas of relating education to science and technology and to the development of the human personality as such. Partly because they considered their own classical learning superior to that of "the natives," and partly because they knew that the "modern" content of their education systems was vitally relevant to the latter's needs, the colonial rulers made little attempt to adjust the imported education systems to those of the indigenous cultures. The British Government's famous decision of 1835 that the Indian upper classes should have an European-type education in the English language, was momentous for the future. The Hindu intellectuals enthusiastically absorbed the ideas of Western science and of British justice and democracy, and then began to ask why the British were not putting them into practice in their governing of India. In introducing their own ideas of the Rights of Man and of science into colonial education systems, the colonial powers were thus unwittingly undermining their own rule.

By the mid-twentieth century, therefore, the developing countries were spotted with a small sprinkling of universities, colleges, secondary and primary schools, some publicly but most privately financed—many were missionary schools—in which a small elite of "the natives" received a Western-type education—from Westerners. The "natives" may have hated the colonial rulers; but they seized eagerly the opportunities offered to enter into the modern world and to gain thereby a wage-paid job. The ultimate goal came to be to complete one's studies in the West. Most of the outstanding leaders of Africa and Asia who grew up before 1939—Gandhi, Nehru, Jinnah and Mrs. Gandhi in India; Chiang Kai-shek and Chou En-lai in China; and Kenyatta, Nkrumah, Nyerere and Kaunda in Africa—had a university education in America or Europe. Most Africans, in fact, had little alternative, for the colonial powers in Africa signally failed to provide facilities for higher education. When the former Belgian Congo attained independence in 1960, "the facilities for secondary education were derisory and there was no Congolese in the administration with a rank above chief clerk and none in the army above an NCO. The Congolese graduates could be counted on the fingers of one hand: there was no Congolese doctor, lawyer or engineer." [1] In the independent countries of Latin America the education systems, based on the Spanish language and the Roman Catholic culture, remained largely self-sufficient and inward-looking.

There was, for instance, almost no research taking place in the universities into the physical or social sciences.[2]

In Asia, the Middle East and Latin America all these institutions, traditional and Western, catered generally to the children of the upper classes, the already literate elite. In classless Africa, although there were far fewer schools and colleges, the children of the peasants had some chance of entering them. In contrast to the situation elsewhere, most of the modern African leaders have come from the villages. Their Western education has given them an understanding of the modern world, but they also have an understanding of village life in their bones. This fact has been of immense importance to their leadership in the sixties. (Gandhi and Nehru had to make the link with the peasants self-consciously, but the fact that they did make it was also of crucial importance to the future of independent India.)

By the mid-twentieth century the coming of European education had not reduced quantitatively the gulf between the literate few and the illiterate masses. About 80 to 85 percent of the Africans, Arabs, Chinese and Indians, and 42 percent of the Latin Americans, were illiterate.[3] But it had provided the slenderest of bridges for the exceptional person to cross the gulf; and at the same time it had changed the gulf, qualitatively, by bringing the elite into the modern world, into a culture outside the experience and comprehension of most illiterates. Thus the masses now tend to attach to the "classical" element in Western education the same charismatic prestige as that formerly accorded to their own classical tradition. To have memorized Shakespeare or Racine or the Bible has become as much a passport to elitism, with all its perquisites of power and privilege, as to have memorized the Hindu Mahabharata or the Muslim Koran.

Since 1945 the leaders of the developing countries have given a very high priority to the *quantitative* expansion of education. In the first place, the painful experiences of colonialism have enhanced their desire for social justice, for the implementation of the right to education affirmed in the United Nations Universal Declaration of Human Rights. (One has only to cast an eye at South Africa and Rhodesia, where over ten times as much money is spent on the education of each white child as on each black child, to understand their feelings.) [4] Second, they know that education is basic to the full deployment of that *human* energy which, according to the United Nations Educational Scientific Cultural Organization (UNESCO), constitutes 80 percent of development resources—an assessment which the achievements of Japan have confirmed. Third, they realize that education is equally basic to the effective expression of political rights. (In Zambia, a few years before independence, a British district commissioner asked a thousand Africans if they knew the meaning of the phrase "one man, one vote." Only three could give him a coherent reply, and they were schoolteachers.) Fourth, they realize that education is an important means of creating national unity. In the classroom children of different tribes, castes, colours and creeds can be taught to identify with one another as citizens of the same nation-state. Finally, there is the insistent demand for education from parents and children. "When one knows how to read, one feels the master of one's destiny," said a Moroccan schoolboy.[5]

The education systems which the leaders sought to expand were, naturally, the existing ones in which they themselves had been raised, with their formal academic curricula. Many countries, in their zeal, directed 25 percent or more of their budgets to education. Since 1960 the education budgets of the poor countries have grown twice as fast as their national incomes. The result has been that, in general, gross enrollments have more than doubled at every level since the mid-fifties—in Africa they have trebled. In 1967–68, primary school enrollment amounted to 70 percent of the age groups in Latin America, 55 percent in Asia (excluding China), and 40 percent in Africa. The comparable figures for secondary education were 35, 30 and 15 percent. (The North American figures are 98 and 92 percent respectively.) [7] Nevertheless, this expansion has only just kept ahead of the population growth.

Some of the rich countries have abetted the policy of expanding existing education systems in the poorer countries as a means of continuing their cultural influence. For example, in 1965 the Francophone countries of Africa were employing some seven thousand French primary and secondary teachers; the French government was paying four-fifths of their salaries. This means that many African children are gaining their education in the French language from French textbooks produced for French children in France.[8] Some of the education systems of the Commonwealth countries are still geared to the British education system; children in countries such as Jamaica, Kenya and Singapore take examinations based on those of the British universities. A reason for continuing these systems after independence is that a person who has had a Western type of education can claim equality and status in the Western world.

The concentration on *quantitative* expansion has had a number of unfortunate results. At the primary level classes are often overcrowded —in Kingston, Jamaica, for example, they contain ninety children or more—and the teachers are undertrained and underpaid. In the French-speaking countries of Africa the teachers have normally had only a primary school education themselves. In Latin America they are often appointed by the priest or mayor—who accordingly sees to it that the teaching upholds the status quo. Sometimes they teach in a foreign language—in many African and Latin American states no textbooks yet exist in the multifarious African and Indian languages. A basic cause of poor results in primary schools may be bad nutrition. An Englishman visiting a primary school in Tanzania found that at least half of a class of thirty-eight children had had no breakfast, and some only a cup of tea. The school was providing a lunch of oatmeal and milk powder, but twenty of the children had not eaten it, because it was provided free only to those whose parents paid a contribution of a dollar a year to school transport. The childrens' dullness in class, which so irritated the young teacher, was caused by hunger, not laziness.[9]

The result of these conditions within the classroom, together with other factors such as inability to pay school fees and failure in examinations, is that millions of children drop out before they have completed the four or five years of schooling which are generally necessary to ensure that there is no fall-back into illiteracy. A UNESCO survey of 1969 showed, for example, a primary school drop-out rate of 50 percent in India, Argentina and Libya, 60 percent in Brazil and Mexico and 80 percent in some African states.[10]

Most African countries have concentrated on expanding primary education. Those of Latin America, Asia and the Middle East have given greater emphasis to the expansion of secondary and higher education, but the secondary schools are the victims of the low standards in the primary schools. According to a Teheran university professor, "The quality of education is worse than weak. Secondary schools accept all candidates, even the most mediocre. I know teachers with 70 students or even more, who have become so discouraged that they have given up teaching their classes. University entrants have been so badly taught that I have seen students writing out their English language lessons phonetically in Arabic script. With such an open secondary education we will never form an active elite." [11] This is typical of the situation in many other countries.

Except in Africa, university education has similarly been hectically expanded. In India, for example, one out of every three secondary school graduates goes on to college. The majority of university students study "arts" subjects, partly because of the high prestige still attached to them, and partly because of the much higher investment required to equip the universities to teach science subjects, and, in many countries, the shortage of science teachers at this level. As in secondary education, the quantitative expansion of university education has also caused standards seriously to fall. Large classes of half-comprehending students listen to lectures whose content is irrelevant to their real lives, and "examinitis" has become a common disease. In the northern half of India student unrest is now so serious that many universities are only teaching for about one hundred days a year.

In Africa the policy of giving first priority to primary education has meant that there are not enough secondary or university graduates to fill existing posts.[12] In many other developing countries the situation is reversed. Higher education expansion has outstripped the development of industry and of sophisticated social services. Ten percent of the graduates of the non-Communist Asian countries are said to be unemployed;[13] in 1971 a third of India's three hundred thousand engineers were estimated to be un- or underemployed.[14] Many graduates in such subjects as medicine, physics and engineering emigrate to the West—half the doctors and more than half the nurses in British hospitals are immigrants from the developing countries. Their Western-type education has not equipped them for the work really needed in their own lands, such as first-aid medicine and "intermediate technology" in the countryside, where there is often an almost total absence of modern facilities and equipment. Many of the students in higher education who are sent to study in the West under the aid programs of the rich countries never return to apply their skills at home.

Unemployed graduates form good guerrilla leaders. The guerrilla revolt which broke out in Sri Lanka in 1971 against the socialist government which was trying to modernize the country was led by some of the ten thousand unemployed graduates.

At all levels, educational opportunities are much greater in the towns than in the countryside, and, except in Latin America, greater for boys than for girls. In Asia (excluding China) and Africa about two-thirds of the students are boys.

Technical and vocational education, obviously basic to development, have likewise been considerably expanded—in India, for example, investment in technical education increased sevenfold between 1951 and 1966—but they have been given, in general, a low priority in relation to academic education. Many Africans, in particular, think that Western experts who are encouraging the adoption of a practical and technical type of education are trying to push them back out of the modern world into second-class citizenship. And much of the technical training which is being provided has itself been of an excessively academic character. Agricultural education, for example, "has often stopped at the farm gate, and has not dealt with the problems of collection, storage, transport and distribution. In Uganda, a three-ton lorry carrying the staple green bananas transports no more than 560 lbs of food. The rest is stems, peeling and water." UNESCO advised the Bolivian Government to establish ten rural colleges; fifty-six were founded, however, "with neither workshops nor equipment, with improvised low quality staff, teaching by repetition or learning by rote"; they were not geared to the fostering of peasant participation in national development.[15]

By the mid-sixties, therefore, there was a growing realization that much of the heroic effort to expand existing education systems quantitatively was being counterproductive, impeding rather than promoting real development. The Third Conference of Ministers of Education and Economic Planning in Asia, held in 1971, recognized that "notwithstanding the progress achieved, the education systems of the Asian countries could not discharge the new duties devolving on them unless all aspects of them were reformed." [16]

Adult education has hitherto been given a low priority. In 1970 nearly half the adults in the world—over 810 million people—were illiterate: 74 percent of the Africans, 47 percent of the Asians (including the Chinese) and 24 percent of the Latin Americans.[17] Illiteracy places a person outside the mental world of the twentieth century, and, especially if his children are going to school, may give him a profound feeling of insecurity. Professor Nazareno Padellaro, former director of the Italian national literacy campaign, wrote, "I, who was born and lived for some time in a region where illiteracy was widespread, remember serene and happy illiterates at peace with themselves and with others. The illiterates whom I know today are aware of being unused and unusable material; rejected, ignored, and involuntary allies of those forces which expel them from civilized society, they try to become even more inert." [18] They are also the people who can be easily aroused to acts of mindless mob violence.

Literacy is the basic foundation for economic and social development. The illiterate person will not be able to read the tax collector's or the money lender's receipt, or the writing on his railway ticket, and so he may be cheated. He will not be able to read the simple instructions which might save his crops from disaster, or the posters which provide basic information about family planning, sanitation and the prevention of disease. A Tunisian phosphate miner who had taken a literacy and vocational training course told a UNESCO official that "before it was as though I were not alive."

In the fifties, the general attitude of governments toward illiteracy was that its elimination would come about automatically within a generation or two as a result of the development of mass popular education for children. This attitude was reinforced by the realization, as the censuses appeared, that half the population of the poor countries was under the age of twenty and that the proportion over forty was fairly low. A "lost generation" of a billion adult illiterates would have to be accepted. UNESCO allotted only a small division to "Adult Education," and the subject was virtually ignored in most national education budgets. Between 1960 and 1970 the adult illiteracy rate in the world diminished by only 4 percent; and because of the population explosion the total number of adult illiterates increased by seventy millions.[19]

By the mid-sixties the dangers of basing economic development on the shaky foundation of adult illiteracy were dawning in the minds of some experts and statesmen. President Nyerere of Tanzania told his Parliament in 1964 that "the first thing to do was to educate the adults. The rising generation's dynamic contribution to the country's economic development would only be felt in 10 or 20 years, while the attitude of adults could make its effects felt immediately. The people should understand the plans made for national development, and be in a position to participate in the necessary changes. Only if they had the ability and will to do so, could the plans succeed." [20]

In Chapter 11 we shall see how UNESCO and some educationalists in the poor countries are thinking out ways of transforming the nature of these education systems, in order to relate them to the development process, as well as to the needs and rights of individuals as such.

References

1. Catherine Hoskyn and Kaye Whiteman, "Congo (Kinshasa)," in *Africa Handbook*, ed. Colin Legum (Middlesex, England: Penguin Books, Ltd., 1969), p. 223.
2. Don Adams and Robert M. Bjork, *Education in Developing Areas* (New York: David McKay Company, Inc., 1969), p. 120.
3. Figures given to the author by UNESCO.
4. Figure given to the author by the Africa Bureau, London.
5. H. M. Phillips, *Literacy and Development* (Paris: UNESCO, 1970), p. 12.
6. Pierre Rondière, "Education . . . But For Whom? . . . And How?" in *UNESCO Courier*, January 1970.
7. Gabriel Carceles Breis, of UNESCO's Office of Statistics, in *UNESCO Courier*, June 1972.
8. Scipio, *Emergent Africa* (London: Chatto and Windus, 1965), pp. 98–119, and René Dumont, *False Start in Africa* (London: Andre Deutsch, 1969), p. 90.
9. Arthur Hopcroft, *Born to Hunger* (London: Pan Books, Ltd., 1968), pp. 13–14.
10. Gabriel Carceles Breis, *op. cit.*
11. Pierre Rondière, *op. cit.*
12. Adam Curle, *Educational Strategy for Developing Countries* (London: Tavistock Publications, Ltd., 1970), p. 138; and Louis François, *The Right to Education: From Proclamation to Achievement 1948–1968* (Paris: UNESCO, 1968), p. 30.
13. Edward Shils, "The Asian Intellectual," in *Asia Handbook*, ed. Guy Wint (New York, N.Y.: Frederick A. Praeger, 1966), p. 598.

14. *The New York Times*, March 3, 1971.

15. Joseph Hutchinson, "Beyond Agriculture," in *Ceres, FAO Review*, Vol. 4, No. 3, May–June 1971, pp. 29–30; and "The Change in Educational Needs of the Developing World," in *The OECD Observer*, No. 53, August 1971, p. 39.

16. Report of the Director-General of UNESCO for 1971 (Paris, 1971), p. 45.

17. Figures given to the author by UNESCO.

18. Mary Burnet, *ABC of Literacy* (Paris: UNESCO, 1965), p. 30.

19. *Breakthrough to Tomorrow* (New York: United Nations Center for Economic and Social Information, 1970), p 52.

20. Louis François, *op. cit.* p. 63.

eight

THE PROBLEM OF HEALTH

As a result of the great advances of medical science, the average length of life has risen considerably in the poor countries in the past twenty-five years. In many African countries, and in India, it is around forty years—nearly double the figure of fifty years ago; in China it is estimated at fifty; many Latin Americans live until their middle fifties; in Mexico the expectation of life is sixty, in Jamaica sixty-four and in Cuba sixty-seven—approaching the average for the rich countries, which is around seventy. The major difference between the rich and the poor countries lies not so much in the length of adult life expectancy as in the fact that many of the inhabitants of the poor countries suffer from chronic bad health all their lives. The contrast may be seen in the main killer diseases. In the rich countries these are heart and cerebrovascular diseases, and cancer. In the poor countries they are essentially enteritis and other diarrheal illnesses, affecting infants in particular; lung illnesses such as pneumonia, bronchitis, influenza and tuberculosis; and parasitic diseases such as malaria and bilharzia.[1]

The major, and interrelated, causes of unhealthiness in the poor countries are malnutrition, infectious diseases, epidemics and bad sanitation. All are related to poverty.

The average North American or Western European consumes in a day perhaps half a pound of meat or fish, an egg and half a pint of milk, together with bread, fruit and vegetables. The daily intake of the average person in India is three-quarters of a pound of cereals, three ounces of milk or milk products and less than one ounce of meat, fish and eggs taken together. The average Nigerian diet consists mainly of starchy roots such as cassava and yams, with some beans and nuts, a little fish and no meat or eggs.

The first of these diets supplies about 80 grams of protein, over half of which is high-quality animal protein, and 3,000 calories; the other diets supply 50 to 60 grams of protein of inferior quality—only 11 percent is animal protein—and 1,800 to 2,400 calories. Two hundred million Americans consume as much animal protein as the one and a half billion people in the poor countries (excluding China). The lesser amount of protein is just about enough to keep a person going, but it provides little margin for emergencies, such as periods of food shortage, or infection, which increase people's needs for protein. The calorie supply in the poor countries is also sufficient to maintain life, but not to provide for a high level of physical activity. In the poor countries as a whole, the picture is not one of widespread starvation, but rather of large numbers of people living at marginal levels of food intake. The food balance figures of the United Nations Food and Agriculture Organization (FAO) show that in many of these countries the total available food supply is just adequate for the theoretical needs of the present population, assuming that distribution is uniform within the community and within the family—an assumption that cannot safely be made. FAO estimates that three hundred to five hundred people in the poor countries do not get enough food, and that one and a half billion do not receive an adequately balanced diet.

Adults who have a low calorie intake lack the energy for hard and prolonged physical work. The lethargy of the inhabitants of tropical countries may be caused as much by shortage of food as by the heat. South African mining companies which recruit labor from developing countries such as Lesotho and Mozambique have found it necessary to feed the men up for several weeks before giving them hard physical work in the mines.

The effects of these shortages are more severe in infants and young children than in adults, because they need extra food in order to grow. The first effect of protein-calorie deficiency is to stop the child's growth. Progressive malnourishment causes him either to die gradually, or to succumb to some infection. Measles, for example, which children in the rich countries take in their stride, is frequently fatal to children in the poor countries. There is as yet no general agreement on an exact definition of malnutrition. The World Health Organization (WHO) classifies any child as undernourished if his body weight is less than seventy-five percent of the average age weight of children of the same age in the rich countries. Its surveys indicate that, on this basis, in many of the poor countries thirty to forty percent of all children below the age of four years are malnourished. It is not surprising that WHO considers malnutrition to be the worst medical problem in the world today.

Further information about the gravity of the problem is provided by mortality statistics. In many of the poor countries the infant mortality rate—deaths in the first year of life per one thousand live births —is one hundred to one fifty—three to five times as high as the rate of about 30 found in West Europe and North America. It has, moreover, recently been realized that the death rates at a somewhat later age—between one and four years—provide an even better index of the nutritional state of a community, because the greatest risk of death from malnutrition arises when the infant is weaned from his mother's breast, and then fed on starchy food at a time when he needs twice as much protein, in terms of body weight, as an adult. In the poor countries the death rates of children between one and four years of age are between five and twenty times as high as in the rich countries. An African word for severe malnutrition is *kwashiorkor,* which means "first-second," i.e., the illness which the first child gets when the second child is born. In Uganda the diet of the first child changes abruptly from milk, rich in protein, to mashed banana. "The results are dramatic. The once happy, healthy baby loses his vitality. His skin and hair become depigmented. His hair may, in fact, go quite grey. His skin cracks, it will not heal, and the cracks become ulcerated. The Kwashiorkor child is listless; he has no exploratory drive and will stay motionless wherever he is placed. Diarrhoea follows and he is unable to retain what food he is given. The stomach and legs swell up with fluid and the muscles waste away. Eventually he dies, death being complicated by gastro-enteritis or broncho-pneumonia." [2]

Childhood malnutrition has profound effects on the well-being of the community. Mothers who are poorly nourished tend to produce small babies. Babies born after a normal duration of pregnancy, but weighing 5½ pounds (2.5 kilograms) are called "small-for-dates." In England about 6 percent of all babies are born small by this definition; in India the proportion is three times as great, presumably because of the malnutrition of the fetus in the womb. Evidence is accumulating that the "small-for-dates" babies have some degree of permanent physical and perhaps also mental handicap. They reach a smaller stature as adults, and they do less well at school than children born of normal size. There is also considerable evidence that children who are malnourished in infancy become retarded mentally. Whether the effects of malnutrition on mental development are permanent and irreparable is not yet known.

We have already discussed the problems of urbanization and unemployment. From the nutritional point of view these phenomena have menacing consequences. As a result of the sophistication of urban life and the need for women to work, traditional breast-feeding practices are being abandoned, and infants are often weaned before three months. The preliminary results of an Inter-American survey of child mortality carried out by the Pan-American Health Organization show a direct connection between the average age of weaning and the death rate. Many of those babies who survive struggle through a period of malnutrition which begins at an earlier age than in rural communities. The brain develops most rapidly during the first six months of life, and its final size has almost been reached by the time the child is one year old. Experimental work on animals shows that permanent effects on the composition and size of the brain are much more serious if malnutrition is imposed at the time of rapid brain growth. The increasing trend toward urbanization, with the consequent earlier onset of malnutrition, may be increasing the numbers of handicapped people, and reducing the "developmental potential" of the community.

It is estimated that at present over three hundred million children in the poor countries are physically retarded; and many of them may also be mentally retarded. A significant proportion of the generation which must mould the future is being rendered incapable of doing so by malnutrition.[3]

Such are the nutritional problems confronting two billion people in the poor countries (excluding China) in the early seventies. What will happen when, by 1985, there are an extra billion mouths in these countries to feed?

Since World War II the governments of the poor countries, with the help of those of the rich countries and of international bodies such as WHO, have made great strides in bringing under control the multifarious epidemic diseases of their largely tropical habitats—many of these diseases are less virulent or are nonexistent in the temperate climates of the rich countries. The eradication of malaria is now regarded as a "pre-investment necessity for development." By 1970 about a billion people—seventy-nine percent of the populations of the world's originally malarious areas—were either covered by malaria eradication programs or freed from the risk of endemic malaria.[4] WHO stated in 1971 that "this has broken the vicious circle of poverty and disease, resulting in ample economic benefits: increased production of rice and wheat because the labor force is able to work." This impressive result, WHO pointed out, was brought about mainly by the use of the pesticide DDT. The most extraordinary development occurred in Sri Lanka, where in the mid-fifties two million people suffered from malaria. By 1963 the use of DDT had reduced the number of victims to seventeen. Spraying was then stopped, for financial reasons. By 1968 there were sixteen thousand cases of malaria, so spraying was resumed. "The safety record of DDT is truly remarkable. At the height of its production 400,000 tons a year were used for agriculture, public health etc. The only confirmed cases of injury (to human life) have been the result of massive accidental or suicidal swallowing of DDT." [5] (We shall note in Chapter 20 the ecological arguments against the use of DDT.) An intensive program for the eradication of smallpox was started in 1967. It was then endemic in 27 countries; by 1968 the number had been reduced to 17, and only two endemic countries had not initiated eradication programs. In West and Central Africa, for example, 100 million out of 120 million inhabitants were vaccinated between 1967 and 1969, and the spread of smallpox was then brought to an end.[6] Other global activities include the international surveillance of the major infectious diseases and the standardization of resistance tests for insecticides—WHO says that there is a "reasonable assurance" that effective vector-borne disease control programs can be carried out despite the resistance phenomenon. Nevertheless, in the late sixties 180 million people were estimated to be afflicted with bilharzia, 250 million with filariasis, 800 million with hookworm, 600 million with trachoma, 50 million with tuberculosis and 10 million with leprosy.[7] Malaria was making a comeback in some areas.

The third problem is that of improving environmental health services. WHO and individual governments of the poor countries have made a major drive in this field, especially in the promotion of clean water supplies and proper sanitation. In 1961 nineteen Latin American countries subscribed to a program to provide water supplies to 70 percent of the urban and 50 percent of the rural population by the end of 1971. Between 1961 and 1967 more than $1.1 billion was invested in the program (40 percent from external sources), and clean water had been brought to fifty-three million people, leaving the needs of sixty-seven million more to be met.[8] In Egypt, since Colonel Nasser's revolution of 1952, clean water supplies have been brought to most of the villages. In spite of the measures taken, however, sanitary conditions remain generally appalling. A survey carried out by WHO in 1962 in seventy-five developing countries showed that 33 percent of the urban population, and less than 10 percent of the rural, had piped water supplies at home; 40 percent of the urban population had no access to any safe water supplies.[9] The shantytowns described in Chapter 6 are sinks of squalor and sickness, including mounting rates of venereal disease.

There are many reasons why the war against ill health is not yet being won. First, in quantitative terms, medical services remain totally inadequate. Whereas in the United States there is one doctor to every 650 persons, and one to every 860 in Britain, in India there is one to every 4,380 persons, in Indonesia one to every 27,560, in Tanzania one to every 40,360 and in Burundi one to every 60,730.[10] A similar situation prevails with regard to the provision of hospitals, clinics, nurses and other medical personnel. As in the case of education, heroic efforts are being made. Many countries are spending more on health services than on any other item except defense. India, for example, is increasing her medical colleges from 51 in 1961 to 103 in 1974.[11] But the population explosion cancels out all quantitative advance.

Second, medical services have usually been developed, as in the West, as specialized organizations, devoted to the cure of disease rather than to its prevention; and they have not been properly integrated into the community life of the masses. This is particularly inappropriate in countries where 45 percent of the population is under the age of fifteen, since at this age the majority of diseases are preventable. The government cannot afford to provide treatment for the peasants in the new prestigious hospitals; the few highly trained doctors usually do not want to work in the rural areas, where there is no equipment and no "civilized" life; and there is an acute shortage of intermediate-level medical personnel to man rural clinics and health centers. In the non-Communist world, rich and poor, the whole question of the organization of medical care to fit the needs of the community is in its infancy.[12]

Third, infectious diseases are being spread around the world by the unprecedented movements of peoples, including the millions of refugees from wars and natural disasters. Some of these diseases, malaria and bilharzia in particular, are apparently being revived and spread as a side result of the enormous irrigation works now being constructed in many parts of the developing world. The mosquitoes which carry the malaria and the snails which house the bilharzia worm breed in the edges of the irrigation channels and the reservoirs (see Chapter 17).

Finally, a fundamental change of attitude may be needed. For centuries people have believed that illness is caused by evil spirits. The following episode illustrates this problem.

When smallpox broke out in a village of Kalahandri district of Orissa State in India, the people knew that the goddess Thalerani was in a rage. The priest, after communicating with the goddess, ordered a sacrifice, followed by a feast. The Government authorities sent a vaccinator. He went from house to house, telling the mothers to bring their babies and children to be vaccinated at once. The women thought him dangerous and closed their doors on him. They called him "the one who makes the babies cry." He was forced, in desperation, to leave the village. The vaccinator and his colleague, the local education officer, then sought the cooperation of the priest. "Gurumaiji" (Revered One), they pleaded with him, "the people have great faith in you. . . . In a disease as serious as smallpox wouldn't you like to offer them medicine as well as religious guidance?" But the priest was indifferent. The next morning, however, he came running toward them. "Please help, please help, my favorite nephew is ill. . . . He is the only son, so you must stay and save him. Give him that medicine that you were telling me about last night." The officials agreed, on condition that the priest cooperate with them. So the priest told the people that the goddess would save only those who were vaccinated with a magic herb. After watching the priest's nephew being vaccinated, the villagers willingly brought their babies, and the priest helped.[13] *

The chronic ill health of the poor countries, and the prevalence of nutrition-deficiency diseases and epidemics, are therefore problems which can only be tackled effectively in the context of environmental and community development. The provision of hospitals, doctors and clinics is not enough. The peoples of the poor countries will not become healthy until the population explosion has been controlled, food supplies of the right nutritional balance increased, public health education expanded, unemployment reduced and welfare services and public amenities provided. But the situation is something of a vicious circle, since the peoples of the poor countries lack the energy to carry out all these developmental tasks while they remain unhealthy.

References

1. *United Nations Demographic Yearbook,* 1970.
2. *Malnutrition in Uganda,* leaflet of the Save the Children Fund, England.
3. This section on malnutrition is based on information supplied by Dr. John Waterlow, C.M.G., Professor of Human Nutrition, School of Tropical Medicine, London University.
4. *WHO Chronicle,* June 1970, pp. 259–63.
5. Quoted in *UNESCO Courier,* February 1972, p. 10.
6. *WHO Chronicle,* June 1970, pp. 259–63.
7. Dr. V. Zammit-Tabona, "Health," in *International Targets for Development,* ed. Richard Symonds (New York: Harper & Row, Inc., 1970), p. 98.
8. *The Second Ten Years of WHO: 1958–67* (Geneva, Switzerland: WHO, 1968), p. 255.
9. *Ibid.*

* Reprinted by permission of Eugene P. Link.

10. *United Nations Statistical Yearbook,* 1969.

11. Planning Commission, Government of India, *Fourth Five Year Plan 1969–74* (Delhi, India: 1970), pp. 388–89.

12. Statement made to the author by Dr. John Waterlow.

13. Abridged from Eugene P. Link and Sushila Mehta, *Victories in the Villages —India* (Plattsburg, N.Y.: State University College, 1964), pp. 33–39.

nine

THE PROBLEMS OF
GOVERNMENT AND DEFENSE

We have seen in Chapter 4 that the very statehood of most of the poor countries does not rest on the same solid foundations as that of most of the rich countries. Within these shaky states government tends to be a shaky affair. Barely a handful of traditional monarchies remain—for example, in 1973, in Saudi Arabia, Jordan, Iran, Afghanistan, Nepal, Thailand and Morocco—whose rulers retain something of the traditional charisma of the divine right of kings. In Latin America the large landowning class still dominates politics in most countries. Increasingly, however, the ruling class is composed of men who have risen from the ranks of the people through the ladders provided by the political and educational systems. Almost everywhere there are constitutions, elections, parliaments and parties. Normally they do not add up to "democracy," but to what might be called plebiscitary dictatorships. In Latin America, where constitutional government has prevailed since the early nineteenth century, a new dictator often produces a new constitution—Venezuela has had twenty-six constitutions since 1830. In most African countries, as in Communist countries, the electors have only one party for which to vote. This ruling party is not, however, normally just a political machine for getting politicians elected, but rather a government-led movement for involving all the people in the processes of administration and development, for breaking down the premodern kinship, caste and religious groups and creating the politically conscious citizens of a modern state. The single ruling party in countries like Egypt, Zambia, Tanzania and Guinea is essentially a *mass* party (in contrast to the Communist Party in Communist countries, which is an elite party), seeking to gain the membership of the majority of the citizens. Where the multiparty system exists, as in most Latin American and some

Asian states, party politics normally is essentially fractious: the parties stand for traditional or interest groups rather than for policies—which must be development policies. (The Congress Party of India combines policies and interests.) Even the local Communist parties have fallen into this pattern, and have thus been able, in multiparty states, to cooperate with non-Communist parties in coalition governments—this has happened, for example, in Chile under the presidency of Dr. Allende, and in the states of Kerala and West Bengal in India. (In Kerala, in 1967, the Communists were leading an electoral alliance of seven parties, which included the anti-Communist Muslim League!) In most countries the executive, whether vested in an American-type presidency—the more general case—or in a British-type premier, is chosen or endorsed by some sort of election. The ruling man or group either manipulates the elections, or seizes power by force and then engineers electoral endorsement. All these parties, parliaments and elections may seem farcical to democratic Westerners; yet their very existence is bringing the peasant into the modern world. (In denying the vote to illiterates—which means mainly to the Indians—some Latin American governments have defaulted on this integrative process.)

There are two main channels for entering the political arena. One is through the parties and the electoral system; the other is through the army, which often offers the poor man almost unique opportunities for advancement. In the majority of countries, where trained civil servants are in very short supply, the army for the time being provides the best administrative machine. Military dictatorship has therefore become the general rule. (India is an exception—see Chapter 11.)

All these regimes want to develop their countries, but several factors make them ill-equipped for this task. The first is their instability. In many of them coups and countercoups take place every few years. In 1971 Bolivia had its 187th military coup in 146 years—the 186th occurred in 1970. If African leaders go on trips abroad, they are liable to find themselves ousted from power when they come home, as happened to Dr. Nkrumah and Dr. Busia of Ghana and Dr. Obote of Uganda. A government which knows that its grip on power is precarious is in a weak position to carry out major reforms and long-term development plans. Hero cults, such as those focused on the former President Nasser of Egypt, on Dr. Castro of Cuba and Mao Tse-tung of China, may be a means of uniting the country in the efforts and sacrifices needed.

A second factor lies in the area of administrative weaknesses—the lack of trained personnel to carry out the numerous tasks of government regulation and control within the mixed economies which most countries are establishing. Economists, statisticians, demographers, business managers, shorthand typists, surveyors and so on are desperately needed. This deficiency is partly the fault of the colonial powers, which simply did not provide the training, and partly the fault of the education systems described in Chapter 7.

A third factor is universal corruption, the bastard child of poverty and premodern social values, which assert that it is a man's moral duty to help any member of his family, tribe or caste in their need. If you are a senior civil servant, how can you refuse to find a job for your starving uncle or fail to award a contract to your unemployed nephew? If you are an underpaid clerk with a host of indigent relatives to support, how can you resist demanding bribes for services performed? All your ancient and traditional ties are to them, and not to that new and more or less meaningless abstraction, the state. And since none of these states, with two exceptions, have yet managed to provide unemployment benefits, old age pensions or free health services for all, to whom can a man turn except his family? In China and Cuba, where welfare states have been established, corruption has also apparently been ended.

Finally, there is the problem of elitism, already discussed in Chapter 6. Good government in a poor country means effective development policies. Such policies imply, as we shall see, not merely the achievement of economic growth through the development of modern industries—normally in the hands of the elites—but also of agrarian and social reforms to deal with the problems discussed in preceding chapters. Unless the elites are prepared to dedicate themselves wholeheartedly to the service of the masses—"Serve the People" is the slogan on the lips of nearly eight hundred million Chinese—it may be impossible to have good government until there has been some form of political revolution. Such a revolution may be born in violence and take an extreme form, as in China and Cuba, or left-wing military regimes may provide the midwives for relatively bloodless social revolution, as has occurred in Egypt and Peru. From 1970 to 1973 Chile presented the unique case of a country in which a democratically elected Marxist president tried to introduce extreme socialist measures, such as the nationalization of *all* industries, through a constitutional system in which nonsocialist or moderate socialist parties flourished freely; the failure of the Chilean experiment in democratic Marxism may provide a continental set-back for "socialism with a human face," as Alexander Dubček of Czechoslovakia called his regime which the Russians so quickly crushed in 1968. It is likely further to polarize the forces of the Right and the Left throughout Latin America.

These basic problems of government inevitably produce an atmosphere of violence and fear. When party rivalry is tribal warfare in disguise, when labor-management confrontation is a modern form of the feudal confrontation between lord and serf, when provinces are threatening to secede, when racial groups have failed to become integrated into "the nation," when contiguous nations are divided by deep-rooted religious or racial tensions—then armed conflict constantly erupts. The sheer mass of social misery and frustration fans the inflammable political situation, producing endemic rioting and guerrilla warfare, whether waged by unemployed university graduates or by landless illiterate peasants. There have been over fifty minor wars in the world since World War II; all of them, with the exception of the Soviet invasions of Hungary in 1956 and Czechoslovakia in 1968, have been fought in the poor countries.

This general condition of violence has, inevitably, a grave impact on internal development. The poor countries are, as a whole, spending more of their meager resources on defense than on any other item —in India, for example, it accounts for a third of the budget.[1] Their defense expenditure is increasing at the rate of 9 or 10 percent a year.[2] Since most of these countries have not yet developed their own armament industries (India, Argentina and Brazil are exceptions),[3] they have to spend on arms imports a high proportion of their small reserves of foreign exchange, which are needed for imports of essential development equipment. Exports of arms from the rich to the poor countries between 1965–69 are estimated to have averaged $2.5 billion a year (of which $300 million went to North and South Vietnam), mainly from the United States, the Soviet Union, Britain and France.[4] The rate of this trade is steadily rising. The "Nixon doctrine" provides that increased military aid should replace the physical presence of American forces in Vietnam and elsewhere. In the fifties most of the arms exports were in the form of "aid"; but during the sixties there was a major thrust by the governments of the rich countries to sell the arms for hard cash, partly in order to get rid of obsolete equipment, and partly to redress an adverse balance of payments. However obsolete they may be in the rich countries, weapons such as jet fighters and surface-to-air missiles may be too sophisticated for the real needs of the poor countries. (In 1958 only four countries received sophisticated aircraft; in 1969, thirty-three.)[5] Sometimes the purchasing country does not possess the trained personnel to use or service the equipment, so that it remains merely a status symbol, or else, as was the case for a time in Egypt, the poor country has to allow an important sector of its economy to be manned by a foreign power, the Soviet Union. (In 1972 the Egyptians terminated Soviet military aid because oil-rich Saudi Arabia agreed to finance Egyptian rearmament.) The poor countries are, nevertheless, as anxious to buy these arms as the rich countries are to sell them. In 1967 the United States Congress imposed a ceiling of $75 million a year on American arms aid and sales to Latin American states, hoping thereby to encourage these states to switch funds to economic development. The result was that they bought $1 billion worth of arms from Canada and Western European countries. In 1971 President Nixon decided that, for the sake of "the security of the United States," the ceiling should be raised.[6] The comment of *The New York Times* was of general relevance: "What does threaten the security of all the hemisphere is an incipient Latin American arms race that will divert scarce resources from desperately needed development efforts, strengthen anti-democratic regimes and increase the danger and potential magnitude of local conflicts. The United States may be powerless to prevent this madness, but there is no good reason why the American taxpayer should be asked to finance it."[7]

Political instability and violence in the poor countries are thus bound up with the problems of poverty, ignorance, disease, unemployment and social and cultural tensions. This instability and violence spark off minor wars which, in the context of the arms race of the rich countries, could ignite a major war. If the rich countries could divert to the poor countries as aid a proportion of the vast sums (over two hundred billion dollars a year—see Chapter 3) which they are spending on their own armaments, this might, paradoxically, prove to be a better investment in their own security.

References

1. Government of India, Ministry of Information, *India, a Reference Annual,* 1970, p. 182.

2. Stockholm International Peace Research Institute Yearbook, 1972, *World Armaments and Disarmament* (New York: Humanities Press, Inc., 1972), p. 53.

3. Stockholm International Peace Research Institute, *The Arms Trade with the Third World* (New York: Humanities Press, Inc., 1971), pp. 723–82.

4. *Ibid.,* p. 11 and p. 7.

5. *Ibid.,* p. 3 and p. 8; and George Thayer, *The War Business* (New York: Simon & Schuster, Inc., 1969), pp. 181–83 and 193–95.

6. *The New York Times,* May 19, 1971.

7. *Ibid.,* May 27, 1971.

ten

INTEGRATED DEVELOPMENT IN CHINA

The Communist regime of China appears to have identified the major internal problems of development more quickly and clearly than almost any other developing country; and it has adopted more or less unique policies to deal with them.

First we must note the historical context within which China's development has taken place. For two thousand years the country was politically united, a great empire throughout which prevailed a lofty culture, expressed in a common public cult, Confucianism, and a common official language and script, underpinning a system of government of immense stability. The emperor ruled, in theory, by moral authority, derived from the "Mandate of Heaven." We saw in Chapter 2 that in all premodern societies the family, caste or kinship group was normally the basic social unit. In China, however, the Confucian scriptures were *essentially* a code prescribing how to maintain harmonious relationships within the family, and within the empire as the "family of families." The government of the "family of families" was highly centralized, and was carried out by a class of scholar-gentry (mandarins), recruited, from about 200 B.C. until A.D. 1905, by competitive examination in the Confucian scriptures. This great and self-sufficient empire regarded itself as superior to all other countries in the world, whose emissaries were treated simply as "barbarians, bearing tribute." The impact of the Western world on China between the Opium Wars of 1839–41 and the Communist Revolution of 1949 was both so humiliating and so limited—since China was only marginally colonized—that apart from technological development, the positive aspects of modern culture, the ideals of the Rights of Man, had little chance to take firm root. The main features of Marxism therefore fit in well with Chinese traditions: its attitude that power should be based on the moral authority of the Marxist scriptures as interpreted by a scholar-ruler of almost godlike stature; its centralized rule through an elite—the Communist Party replacing the mandarins; and its affirmation that the purpose of the individual's life is not to express his own personality but to serve the group. Marxism is also relevant to China's contemporary needs. Confucianism looked back toward a Golden Age in the past. Marxism rejects the past and provides the Chinese, for the first time, with the hope of progressing toward a Golden Age in the future. Marxism also enables the Chinese to heap moral condemnation on the wicked capitalist West which humiliated them in the past, while at the same time adopting Western science and technology—since it claims to be an essentially "scientific" system of thought.

In 1949, when the Communists came to power, the huge country was not only undeveloped, but had been devastated by half a century of civil and foreign war, during the course of which perhaps some fifty million people lost their lives. We have already seen how the peasants, who formed over 80 percent of the population, and who were generally illiterate, were in the grip of the feudalistic landlords and of the money lenders. Agriculture was stagnant and unstable; in one year in the thirties floods and the ensuing famine caused the death of ten million people. The limited prewar industrial development, largely in the coastal areas, promoted and financed by foreign capitalists in their own interests, had been smashed during the war with the Japanese (1937–45). In 1945, 70 percent of China's most developed industry was in Manchuria. In general China was industrially "a sheet of blank paper," as Mao Tse-tung put it. Its mineral resources were largely unexplored. Its railway system, also built by foreign capital, was designed to serve the east coast industries. The vast regions of the northwest and the southwest contained less than eight hundred kilometers of railway.[1] The peasant's life was haunted by insecurity: by chronic famines due to floods and droughts; by ill health—there were only twenty thousand doctors in the whole country in 1950; by fear of the rough and brutal soldiery who fought over his fields, and of the machinations of evil spirits. Many were reduced—as they had been periodically through the centuries—to eating grass, to selling their daughters into prostitution, to sharing one suit of clothes around the family. The corrupt and cruel dictatorship of Chiang Kai-shek did nothing effective for them. And over the whole scene stalked the specter of inflation—the yuan, declared in August, 1948, to be worth twenty-five American cents, passed the one-million-dollar mark in January, 1949, bringing trade to a standstill.[2]

Western journalists who returned to China in 1971 found a very different scene.

"The improvement in the physical condition of the people since the Communist take-over in 1949 is staggering. The hordes of beggars and of the starving and diseased that once were familiar are gone. The people look healthy and are obviously adequately fed and clad, although there is uniform dullness in the blue and grey tunics over inevitable baggy pants. . . . The state assures each family a basic income sufficient to feed and house itself. Living standards . . . seem uniformly adequate in the Asian context. The writer wandered unescorted down some back streets and village lanes without seeing sanitary conditions as bad as in New York ghettos." [3]

The country is now covered with irrigation projects, large and small, employing the labor of some fifty million people. Forty-six dams are planned for the Yellow River alone, of which nine are in operation or under construction.[4] Fertilizer plants are springing up all over the country. The area under forests, terribly denuded in the past, is being doubled under the "Make China Green" program. Seed is being sown by airplane in eroded areas. Tractors and other machines are being used in the fields side by side with human and animal muscle power. Because of these and other measures the Chinese peasant is, probably for the first time in history, eating his fill—"for him the victory of victories." In 1972 Premier Chou En-lai stated that grain production had increased from 160 million tons in 1961 to 240 million tons in 1970, though it fell to 240 million tons in 1972 because of exceptional droughts.[5] And since yields per acre are still relatively low—rice yields are stated to be about half those of Japan and Taiwan —with further expansion of irrigation and of fertilizer supplies, and of the use of improved seeds (the journalists found that the Chinese had not yet heard of the "Green Revolution," but were developing their own new seed strains)[6] the prospects for increasing China's food supplies are good. Such increase will be essential not only to raise nutrition standards, but also to feed the twelve to fifteen million extra mouths born each year, and to provide exports to pay for the import of sophisticated machinery. (In 1969 China exported eight hundred thousand tons of rice, 1 percent of its crop.)[7] Meanwhile, the average peasant knows that stocks of grain have been established throughout the country, so that if crops fail in one year or in one place he will not starve—this stockpiling has been facilitated by the import of about five million tons of wheat a year from the Western world to feed the coastal towns. There were no reports of massive starvation when the harvests failed badly for the three years

1958–60 in succession. Famines may be a thing of the past in China. The industrial scene has also been transformed. The urban population is estimated to have risen from 50 to 150 million between 1949 and 1971.[8] China is now making most of the machinery she needs, from tractors to rockets. Huge industrial complexes have sprung up, not only in the accessible coastal regions, but also in the remote western and northern areas of the country. These are complemented by medium and small industries dispersed over the countryside, factory chimneys rising from the fields, and fields interspersed in the factory areas. The raw materials for this industry are being produced within China. Whereas there were only 200 geologists in the country in 1949, there are now 21,000 geological workers, helped by 400 more highly trained specialists from other socialist countries. They have discovered vast reserves of coal, iron, oil, tungsten, tin, nickel and other minerals. China has the mineral wealth to become a first-class power, and is rapidly developing the technology to exploit this wealth.[9]

Industrial and agricultural development are being facilitated by a transport revolution. Railways are linking most regions of the country in a "web of steel"; roads are being built over passes fourteen thousand feet high; canals are providing water transport between river basins. Internal air travel is expanding. "Across the broad Yangtze River near Nanking, there is a new two-level bridge, almost 10 miles long, which some foreign experts doubted could ever be built. It was completed in eight years with as many as 50,000 people working in a single day, carrying earth in baskets on their heads." [10]

Balanced budgets and state control of wages, prices and interest rates have controlled inflation and stabilized the currency. (In 1971 the official exchange rate of the yuan was 2.4 to the dollar.)

Everyone is employed, men and women working side by side for equal pay in the similar clothes which symbolize their equality. " 'In the old society we were fired if we got married or had a child, but here we get 56 to 72 days of paid maternity leave and special rest periods for the first seven months after returning to the job,' Mrs. Chang Wen-lan, a 45-year-old worker, said." [11] Since the Cultural Revolution of 1966 (see below) great numbers of surplus workers have been moved from the towns into the villages—nearly a million from Shanghai alone. Almost all children are in school, and most adults are becoming literate on the basis of simplified characters introduced by the Communists. (In 1972 Mao was urging the introduction of the Roman alphabet, which would make it far easier for ordinary people to become literate.) In 1971 the authorities claimed that illiteracy had been reduced from 70 to 80 percent in 1949 to 10 percent. Homes, usually of two rooms, with a shared kitchen, are provided with the jobs, at cheap rents—3 or 5 percent of income. The shops are well stocked with basic consumer goods, although bread and cotton cloth are rationed, the latter to one suit of clothes a year. Most people have access to health clinics where simple ailments are dealt with at the nominal cost of one yuan a year by semiqualified health workers, and fairly easy access to hospitals for more serious illnesses, where treatment is free. There are kindergartens for the little children and "homes of respect" for the aged. Minimum per capita incomes have been fixed in each region of the country, and when family income falls below this minimum, the community—the factory or the commune (see below)—makes up the difference. Women can retire at fifty and men at sixty on a pension equivalent to 70 percent of their earned income. China is the only major poor country which has succeeded in establishing the basic services of the welfare state for all its citizens.

Everywhere that the journalists went, they found that the average family consisted of two or three children. Mrs. Hu, the thirty-five-year-old leader of a production team in the Machiao commune near Shanghai, told them, "The old idea that parents should have lots of children to honour and support them is finished." [12] The state encourages young people not to marry till their late twenties, provides free contraceptives, abortions and sterilization, and withholds ration cards for children above the fourth. As a result the population growth rate was estimated in 1972 to have fallen to 1.7 percent. "The central problem of the economy"—the problem of relating food supplies and industrial production to population—"now seems within reach of a solution." [13]

Up to 1960 the Russians gave the Chinese substantial development aid: loans, equipment and experts. But when the quarrel between the two Communist giants developed they withdrew it all, and China has repaid every cent received. Apart from this, China has received only small-scale aid from the Communist countries of Eastern Europe. It has purchased equipment from Western Europe and Japan.[14]

How have the Chinese achieved this economic and social transformation?

Communist China is, like the Soviet Union, a completely socialist state. All the "means of production, distribution and exchange" are publicly owned, except for the small private plots which the peasants are allowed to keep, enough to grow vegetables on and to provide for a pig and a hen or two; and there is comprehensive and mandatory planning. In China, as in the Soviet Union, political power is vested in the Communist Party. There is, however, a fundamental difference between the two Communist systems. In accordance with the precepts of Marxism, the Soviet system sought from the first to base itself on the support of the urban proletariat. The peasants were regarded as an apolitical conservative force, and were dragooned into the system by Stalin in the thirties at the cost of some ten million deaths. Mao Tse-tung realized in the mid-twenties that the peasants were the potential revolutionary force in China—"like a tornado or tempest—a force so extraordinarily swift and violent that no power, however great, can suppress it," he called them.[15] In the twenty-year struggle with the Kuomintang and the Japanese which preceded the Communist seizure of power in 1949, he stirred up the tornado by developing it as a guerrilla force. Throughout his rule he has always put the peasants first.

Three facts must be noted about the government of Communist China. First, it has given the country over twenty years of peaceful and firm rule after half a century of incessant warfare. Second, it is based on the principle of mass participation. Before 1949 the people did not participate in the political process at all. Central and local government was carried out by a class of centrally appointed officials—after the collapse of the empire in 1911 the mandarinate continued in a modified form. Now the whole country is covered with a network of councils and congresses: those of the administration, which deal with practical matters, and those of the Party, which deal with policy and ideology, the two systems interlocking. The councils are organized in a descending hierarchy, from the State Council of the administration and the Central Committee of the Party at the top, headed by Premier Chou En-lai and Chairman Mao respectively, to administrative "revolutionary committees" and Party cells at the bottom. The members of all these bodies are chosen, not by voting between rival candidates, but by reaching a consensus among the electors after discussion,[16] though the revolutionary committees, established during the Cultural Revolution, include members of the armed forces.[17] Throughout the hierarchy of councils there is a continuous two-way flow, ideas and suggestions flowing upwards from the people, and decisions and orders flowing downwards from the rulers. The aim is "to bind the bottom to the top," to secure the active participation of the masses in the policies formulated by the leaders. Third, standards of honesty and austerity have been set by the leaders and inculcated at every level.[18] Elimination of the debilitating corruption of the past has been achieved partly by replacing the ancient ethic of loyalty to the extended family by that of loyalty to the Party group, and partly by the simple fact that the old, the sick and the helpless are cared for by the state.

These characteristics of the Chinese system of government exist, in theory at least, in the Soviet model. But from this point Mao's attitude to the peasants has inspired a radical new departure. In the Soviet Union, as in the Western world, agriculture, industry, health services, education, taxation, judicial matters, military service and the system of administration are all organized as national services, involving, inevitably, much bureaucracy, centralization and specialization. In the developing countries in general, the attempt to imitate this system has fostered the dangerous internal gulfs to which we referred in previous chapters: between the cities and the villages; between industry and agriculture; between the educated and the illiterate; and between the rich elite who can afford to live and think like the people in the Western world, and the masses who are still sunk in poverty and who think in premodern terms. The determination to prevent or eliminate these gulfs in China has produced a unique institution: the commune. In 1958 the Central Committee of the Chinese Communist Party announced that "a new social organisation [has] appeared fresh as the morning sun above the broad horizon of East Asia"; the commune would now be "the basic unit of the socialist structure of our country." [19]

The commune is first of all a unit of landownership. When the Communists came to power they eliminated the old landlords without compensation—some hundreds of thousands were executed, the rest turned into laborers—and then gave the peasants some 110 million acres in private ownership. The next step was to coax the peasants into the collective ownership of some 740,000 "advanced cooperatives," in which 100 to 300 families owned the land collectively.[20] These cooperatives were then amalgamated into communes, which by 1970 numbered over 70,000,[21] with populations ranging from a few thousand to about 70,000.[22] The commune differs from the "advanced cooperative," or the collective and state farms of the Soviet Union, in that it is a self-governing unit for all the main services of life. It has a network of hospitals, health centers, kindergartens, elementary, secondary and technical schools, laundries, cafeterias, grain mills, electricity and water stations and small industries. Through it the peasant citizen is provided with the "Five Basic Guarantees": food, clothing, shelter, medical care and funeral expenses. Each commune, like each urban factory, has a fund for the relief of the needy, into which the workers pay 2 percent of their earnings.

Certain features of the communes may be noted. First, for cultivation the big unit is broken down into "production teams" of twenty or thirty families, the equivalent of one village, and of "brigades" consisting of eight or ten teams. On the ground level, therefore, the groups are kept small enough for human intimacy. Second, the peasants own their own homes, and also the small plots to which we have referred. Third, the communes manage their own finances; the workers are not wage laborers of the state, as in the factories and the state farms of the Soviet Union. Half the income is usually distributed among the workers, who are paid according to skill, physical ability, ideological development and number of years they have worked. The other half is set aside to meet communal running costs, and state rents and taxes, and to provide for capital investment, which may amount to 5 to 12 percent of the commune's resources. "This steady investment in the production and welfare infrastructure of the Chinese countryside is unparalleled in any other developing country." [23] Fourth, the commune is a technological unit. Its members are encouraged to develop a range of small industries, through their own efforts, on the basis of "intermediate technology." In the "Great Leap Forward" of 1958 the peasants set up two million primitive iron-smelting furnaces in their back yards. These proved to be unproductive, and the experiment was soon abandoned. But it left a residue of "steel consciousness," and prepared the way for more sensible experimentation. In the various groups to which he belongs, in the factory, farm and school, every Chinese is encouraged to put forward technical ideas. The *People's Daily* of March 21, 1960, reported that "when the Party Committee of I-cheng County in Shansi Province called an 'increase production' meeting of the Party cadres engaged in factories and mines under its control, more than 15,000 suggestions were said to have been listed, over 10,000 of which were referred for serious study. Ultimately, after testing by 'technical innovation teams,' just under 7,000 were adopted." [24] Since the Cultural Revolution each factory keeps an official count of the number of innovations introduced by workers. [25] Mao Tse-tung recently wrote that "after reading in the People's Daily of how schistomomiasis"—China's most serious health problem—"was wiped out in Yukiang County"—by storing human excrement used for fertilizer, covering it with mud and allowing it to ferment long enough to kill all the parasites, "so many fancies crossed my mind that I could not sleep. In the warm morning breeze, as the sunlight fell on my window, I looked towards the distant southern sky and in my happiness wrote the following lines"—a poem. [26] The communes are developing a vast reservoir of ground-level amateur technicians, and also producing simple consumer goods to serve as incentives to its peasants to increase agricultural production. Finally, the commune is the key local government area, to which many functions have been delegated by the traditional province, which covers about 200,000 people. Thus formal government is brought closer to the people and also integrated with economic production. [27]

Overspanning the communes is the central government, reserving to itself the rights of overall planning (though plans are submitted to Party committees, revolutionary committees and workers on the factory floor for discussion) and the responsibility for such matters as national investment in major projects, foreign trade and wage policies. The government's economic policy is summed up in two slogans. The first is: "Agriculture is the base of the national economy, with industry as the leading factor." The Chinese government, like those of most developing countries, initially gave first priority to heavy industry; but the three disastrous harvests of 1958–61 led it to change the emphasis. The second slogan is: "Walking on Two Legs." One leg is the development of large, sophisticated industries and engineering complexes; the other is the complementary development of the little do-it-yourself enterprises.

We must now glance at the psychology of Communist ideology in China. Marxism has often been called a secular religion, because it aims at creating a new man, who will inhabit a new and higher kind of society, redeemed from the sins of materialism and profit-seeking which corrupt the capitalist world. According to the Chinese, the Soviet comrades have relapsed into "revisionism." The Soviet new man is not a redeemed person, a true "Communist," but simply a bureaucrat or technocrat of a society based on state capitalism. Thus there is emerging in the Soviet Union a "new class" of Communist mandarins, of new elites, divorced from the masses of the proletariat. In China the dangers of revisionism are enhanced by the existence of well-established universities with ancient scholastic traditions of immense prestige, concerned, until 1966, partly with transmitting the traditional culture and partly with inculcating the liberalism and science of the West. The Cultural Revolution of 1966–69 seems to have been inspired by Mao's determination to eliminate these dangers. Hence it involved a two-pronged attack on the university professors and traditional curriculum, on the one hand, and on the Communist bureaucracy on the other.

The universities were closed for four years. The specialists they produced, such as highly trained doctors, were described by Mao as "cripples without crutches" [28]—people who would have no scope to practice their specialization in the primitive conditions of the countryside. Mao determined that education should now be geared toward training to "serve the people." Everyone, from the primary school child to the senior diplomat, is to learn in practice what this service means through regular spells of work in factory and field. The length of school life has been reduced from twelve years to nine or ten, middle school education being almost universal.[29] After a few years of ordinary work a young person may apply to be elected by his fellows to go to college. The basic criteria for acceptance are physical fitness and political soundness; but entrance examinations, abolished in 1966, have been restored. Selected workers, peasants and soldiers have been incorporated into the teaching staff, college presidents replaced by revolutionary committees, and theoretical instruction integrated with practical work by coupling each campus with a particular factory or commune. After the shortened course of two or three years most of the students return to the factories or the fields. The highly qualified specialists whom the country needs are still being trained, but they are being supplemented by large numbers of short-term trainees such as the "barefoot doctors" who treat common illnesses in the communes.

For some the Cultural Revolution has been a traumatic experience. Many scholarly and sensitive personalities were assaulted and humiliated by gangs of fanatical Red Guard youths (see below); and hundreds of thousands of educated people, especially those who had absorbed Western ideas, have been exiled to peasant life in the villages.

The integration of the education system into the economic life of the country has been complemented by the integration of the army into the educational system. In May 1966 Mao issued a directive "calling on the army to transform itself into a vast school for learning not only military, but also political and cultural affairs. It should be capable of engaging in agricultural and industrial production, in mass work, and in the constant criticism of exploitative classes and ideas." [30]

The second aim of the Cultural Revolution was to transform the bureaucracy, to eliminate or re-educate "Party persons in authority," or "Rightists," who were accused of "carrying out their work in an authoritarian manner, developing a superior attitude to the workers, forming gangs to protect each other, and taking advantage of their position to gain privilege and amenities for themselves." [31] This did not mean, in principle, the purging of individuals deemed to be hostile to the ruling clique, as in Stalin's ferocious purges in Russia. It was, rather, an attempt to break down the political tradition of centuries, inculcated by religion, which had trained the masses to submit dutifully to the authority of their superiors. In a Resolution of August 1966 the Central Committee of the Party called upon the Party leadership to "put daring above everything else and boldly arouse the masses," and the masses to educate themselves to discuss, and to take initiatives. "The method to be used in debates is to present the facts, reason things out, and persuade through reasoning," not "by coercion or force." [32] The result was a mass movement in which the Party officials (cadres) and administrators, including top men, were questioned and criticized. At every level there were drastic bureaucratic reductions; Premier Chou En-lai claimed that the central government personnel had been reduced from sixty thousand to ten thousand.[33] In September 1973 a number of senior ministerial posts were still vacant.

The movement to eliminate elitism in the education system and in the bureaucracy was accompanied by cultural iconoclasm—the campaign to eliminate the "Four Olds—Old Things, Old Ideas, Old Customs, Old Habits." One American journalist reported: "In not a single room seen by the writer was there any family altar, any tablets to ancestors or any representation of the old gods formerly worshipped by the Chinese masses. In as Westernized a city as Hong Kong . . . such things are still commonplace in Chinese homes.[34]

In order to carry out the Cultural Revolution in these fields, Mao mobilized China's youth in the "Red Guards." Bands of school children, students from the closed-down universities and young workers were brought from far and wide into the big cities, where they "swept through the streets, . . . yelling 'down with the Four Olds' . . . and changing street names, ripping down shop signs, boarding up the doors of churches and temples. . . ."[35] Many spent endless hours interrogating officials, Party cadres, teachers and factory managers. Others, incapable of responding to the Party's injunction to work by peaceful persuasion, were swept away by hysterical fanaticism or sheer hooliganism. The army was then called in to curb the Red Guards and keep the discussions at a peaceful level, and "Ultra-Leftism" was as severely condemned as "Rightism." By 1969 the children and students were back in their classrooms, and the adults, including many of the people in responsible positions who had been interrogated, were back at their jobs. Revolutionary committees representing the workers, management, Party and armed forces had been established in every production and political unit in China.[36] A field exercise in anti-authoritarianism had been carried out. China was beginning to grapple with one of the key questions of the modern world: how to secure the active participation of the masses in decisions of policy about the complex economic, technical and political issues of development.

The ethos of the rich countries of the Western world is to stimulate people to work for growth by offering them material incentives, and to encourage popular participation by providing a secular education which seeks to develop the individual according to his "age, aptitude and ability" (British Education Act of 1944). "Sick" societies of "alienated" people have resulted, because one vital ingredient has been lacking: the emotional force of a shared ideal. Mao Tse-tung has sought to make idealism the motive force for development, an idealism focused by worshipping him as the exemplar of his ideals, which most Chinese study in his written "Thoughts" as devoutly as a committed Christian studies his Bible. "When an official told me the ideology of a worker was considered as important as his output and seniority in fixing his wage, I asked what would happen if the best producer in the plant said he did not believe in Mao thought. 'But that is impossible,' he replied. 'It couldn't happen. If he didn't believe in Mao's thought he couldn't be a good worker.' " [37] The new fifteen-mile-long Peking subway has "16 palatial stations, all built of different colored marble from Yunnan. No two stations are alike in lighting, construction and color. . . . 'In building the subway,' the commandant said, 'the workers, in accordance with Chairman Mao's instructions, displayed courage and studied Mao Tse-tung's thoughts to overcome the difficulties.' " [38] But one of the implications of Mao's Cultural Revolution is that he himself is now criticizing the Mao "personality cult" as "extravagant and importunate." [39] If the Chinese cease to rely for guidance on Mao's thoughts, to whose will they turn? To their own?

The Chinese seem to be solving some of the gravest problems with which most of the developing countries are grappling. This massive achievement has been made possible by the willingness to save—that is, to work hard and at the same time to forgo all but the barest minimum of consumer goods—and to accept a totalitarian system which denies them personal freedom—which they never experienced anyway in their past history. The rulers have fostered this willingness by playing down materialistic motives and stimulating the fervent and naïve idealism of simple people; and by promoting the active *participation* of everyone within the framework of the system. The leaders seem to have succeeded in canalizing the hitherto untapped energies of the Chinese masses. They have deployed their own interpretation of Marxist ideology to marry their ancient traditions of rule by moral authority from above, of a centralized state based on harmonious relationships and dedicated service, to the modern ideals of technological progress and social rights for the masses. But the necessary price has been the discouragement of the other Rights of Man, above all, of individual self-expression and the individual's right to make his personal judgment and conscience the final arbiter of his decisions. (Eight models have been provided by the authorities for the artistic expression of eight hundred million people. They comprise four operas, two ballets, one symphony and one piece of proletarian sculpture.)[40] By educating millions of fresh young minds—who have not experienced the suffering and the drama of the "preliberation" period—in objective scientific thinking; by inculcating active participation and self-criticism; by replacing family loyalties with the more impersonal loyalties to the Party and the state and by liberating women, the Chinese leaders may be setting fuses under their own authoritarian system. A society which, however dogmatic its attitudes, believes fundamentally in progress, cannot stand still. In fact, the degrading of the elites on whose intellectual development the progress of the country must largely rely may be a step backwards which will have to be retraced. Further great changes may be expected in due course in China. And the process of full "modernization" is likely to be accelerated by its sudden emergence from age-old isolation into the arena of international affairs. A portent for the future is the Chinese Government's decision in 1972 to engage three American companies to develop a system of satellite-beamed telecommunications circuits which will put China into television and telephone contact with sixty nations.[41]

References

1. Keith Buchanan, *The Transformation of the Chinese Earth* (London: G. Bell and Sons, Ltd., 1970), p. 252.

2. Dennis Bloodworth, *Chinese Looking Glass* (Middlesex, England: Penguin Books, Ltd., 1969), p. 352.

3. Seymour Topping, "New Dogma, New Marxist Man," in *The New York Times Report From Red China* (New York: New York Times Co. Quadrangle Books, 1971), p. 261.

4. Buchanan, *op. cit.*, p. 195.

5. Statement by Premier Chou En-lai, reported in *The Manchester Guardian Weekly*, December 2, 1972.

6. Tillman Durdin, "New Grains Increase Yields on Farms," in *The New York Times Report From Red China, op. cit.*, p. 209.

7. Ralph W. Huenemann, "Agriculture and Rural Development," in *A Century of Struggle: Canadian Essays on Revolutionary China*, ed. J. M. Gibson and D. M. Johnson (Toronto, Canada: The Canadian Institute of International Affairs, 1971), p. 92.

8. Thomas G. Rawski, "Trade, Industry and Urban Development," in *A Century of Struggle: Canadian Essays on Revolutionary China, op. cit.*, p. 94.

9. Buchanan, *op. cit.*, p. 218.

10. Seymour Topping, "Mass Efforts Achieve Great Feats," in *The New York Times Report From Red China, op. cit.*, p. 219.

11. Seymour Topping, "Welfare Plan Assures Minimum Living Standard," in *The New York Times Report From Red China, op. cit.*, p. 190.

12. Tillman Durdin, "The Birth Rate is Cut in New Society," in *The New York Times Report From Red China, op. cit.*, p. 192.

13. Seymour Topping, "Economic Policy Stresses Local Self-Help," in *The New York Times Report From Red China, op. cit.*, p. 216.

14. Robert F. Dernberger, "Economic Realities and China's Political Economics," in *China After the Cultural Revolution: A Selection From the Bulletin of the Atomic Scientists* (New York: Random House, 1969), p. 90.

15. Stuart S. Schramm, "Mao and Maoism," in *A Century of Struggle: Canadian Essays on Revolutionary China, op. cit.,* p. 121.

16. Information from Dr. Paul Pickowicz of Wisconsin University.

17. Tillman Durdin, "After the Purges, Order and Stability," in *The New York Times Report From Red China, op. cit.,* p. 176.

18. See Ilsa Sharp, "Travelling into the Flowering Middle Kingdom," in *The Atlantic Monthly,* October 1971, p. 20.

19. Dick Wilson, *A Quarter of Mankind: An Anatomy of China Today* (Middlesex, England: Penguin Books, Ltd., 1968), p. 34.

20. Huenemann, *op. cit.,* pp. 88–89.

21. E. L. Wheelwright and Bruce McFarlane, *The Chinese Road to Socialism* (New York: Monthly Review Press, 1970), p. 181.

22. Information from Dr. Paul Pickowicz.

23. Buchanan, *op. cit.,* pp. 130–38.

24. K. E. Priestley, *Workers of China* (London: Ampersand Press, 1964), p. 30.

25. Seymour Topping, "Economic Policy Stresses Local Self-Help," in *The New York Times Report From Red China, op. cit.,* p. 218.

26. Sally Reston, "Mao's Poem Urges Drive on Snail Fever," in *The New York Times Report From Red China, op. cit.,* pp. 312–13.

27. Edgar Wickberg, "The Peasant and Politics in Revolutionary Times," in *A Century of Struggle, Canadian Essays on Revolutionary China, op. cit.,* p. 51.

28. C. G. H. Oldham, "Science Travels the Maoist Road," in *China After the Cultural Revolution, op. cit.,* p. 226.

29. See: Ross Terrill, "The 800,000,000: Report from China," in *The Atlantic Monthly,* November 1971, pp. 111–17; Paul T. K. Lin, "The Education Revolution," in *A Century of Struggle: Canadian Essays on Revolutionary China, op. cit.,* pp. 65–76; and Tillman Durdin, "Schools Retain Many Conventional Subjects," in *The New York Times Report From Red China, op. cit.,* pp. 280–82.

30. Lin, *op. cit.,* p. 72.

31. Joan Robinson, *The Cultural Revolution in China* (Middlesex, England: Pelican Books, 1969, reprinted 1970), p. 14.

32. *Ibid.,* p. 87 and p. 90.

33. Seymour Topping, "Economic Policy Stresses Self-Help," *op. cit.,* p. 218.

34. Tillman Durdin in *The New York Times,* May 19, 1971.

35. Neil G. Burton, "The Great Proletarian Cultural Revolution," in *A Century of Struggle: Canadian Essays on Revolutionary China, op. cit.,* pp. 111–12.

36. Ross Terrill, *op. cit.,* pp. 107–8; Burton, *op. cit.,* pp. 103–116; Seymour Topping, "Revolutionary Committees Ensure Discipline," in *The New York Times Report From Red China, op. cit.,* pp. 251–54.

37. Tillman Durdin, "Hearing the Works in Person Makes a Difference," in *The New York Times Report From Red China, op. cit.,* p. 173.

38. Audrey Topping, "In Peking, A Subway Ride is Fun," in *The New York Times Report From Red China, op. cit.,* pp. 201–2.

39. Robert Guillan of, "Le Monde," in *The Sunday Times* (London), August 6, 1972.

40. Roxane Witke, "Eye Witness Report: An American Scholar Visits in China," in *Center Report* (Santa Barbara, California: Center for the Study of Democratic Institutions), December 1972, p. 25.

41. *The New York Times,* January 5, 1973.

eleven

INTEGRATED DEVELOPMENT IN OTHER POOR COUNTRIES

With the exception of Cuba, North Vietnam and North Korea, no poor country has established a Communist regime, in the sense of the complete nationalization of productive enterprises (and in Cuba there is still a private sector) and of government through a monolithic Communist Party inspired by Marxism. Virtually none of the poor countries, therefore, have adopted the Chinese model. One major reason is that many countries in Latin America, and some in Asia and the Middle East, are ruled by a landowning class culturally identified with the West, and it may require a revolutionary upheaval to substitute regimes which will provide social justice for the peasants and workers. There is another reason, however, of a more positive nature. Many of these countries have produced idealistic and dedicated leaders who are deliberately seeking a philosophic basis for their new society which is neither an inept imitation of the Western world, nor grounded on Marxism. President Nasser of Egypt told a British journalist in 1961 that "You are making the same mistake about him [President Sekou Touré of Guinea] that you made about us. We are forming a new society which is not capitalist or communist." And President Nyerere of Tanzania has said that Marxism has no relevance to African conditions because it is the product of nineteenth-century industrial Europe.

These new philosophies are still in the process of being worked out, both in theory and in practice; but certain common ingredients can be discerned. First, they reject the negative values of the Western world—its obsession with material prosperity and its aggressive and competitive individualism. Second, they seek to affirm the permanently relevant elements in their own religious and social traditions: the Hindu and Buddhist ideals of *ahimsa*—love, harmlessness, soul force, nonviolence—and *satyagraha*—"firmness in truth"—which Gandhi sought to embody in political action (Gandhi's example has profoundly influenced some of the leaders of the poor countries, especially in Africa); the Muslim's sense of man's utter dependence on God and of the importance of leading a life of moral integrity and personal purity; and the traditional African "communitarianism," in which the individual develops his potential, according to President Léopold Senghor of Senegal, "in and by society, in union with all other beings in the universe, God, animal, tree and pebble." Third, they are trying to relate these traditional ideas to the positive values of the Western world: the humanitarian ideals of the Rights of Man—though social rights may have to take precedence over political and personal rights—and to the objectivity and rationality of science.

In India the Congress Party, which led the independence movement and which has since ruled India through free, democratic elections, has sought to give expression to this new kind of philosophy. In the Middle East and in Africa it is expressed in such terms as "Arab Socialism" and *Ujamaa,* or "familyhood."

These movements are essentially pragmatic and undogmatic. They reject alike Marxist dogma and the dogmatism of the traditional religions. For dogma divides, and they seek to unite. According to President Nyerere, "The foundation, and the objective, of African socialism is the extended family. The true African socialist does not look on one class of men as his brothers and another as his natural enemies." The concept of the brotherhood of man is basic to Islam; and Gandhi spent his life trying to break down the barriers of caste, sect, race and sex. Affirmation of spiritual values therefore underpins these new philosophies. Thus, far from clashing with Western ideals and attitudes, they add a new dimension to them. They point toward the goal of universal brotherhood or world community without asserting, as Marxism does, that this can be achieved only by eliminating a wicked enemy through violent revolution, or, at best, coexisting peacefully with him until he collapses of his own decadence.

Latin America falls largely outside this movement. The institutionalized Roman Catholic Church is still largely tied up with the landowning establishment. But within its ranks a new movement is developing of priests such as Archbishop Helder Camara of Olinda and Recife in Brazil, who are urging that Christianity should express itself in social reform. Some are even joining the peasant guerrillas, like Father Camillo Torres of Colombia, who was killed by the police and has become something of an international martyr.

This pragmatic philosophy of brotherhood, together with natural motives of self-interest, mean that the majority of the poor countries want to develop in partnership with the rich countries. To the extent that the latter can enter into the spirit of this partnership, their contribution is of vital importance. But in putting their own interests first in their relationships with the poor countries, they are often distorting the development of these indigenous philosophies, or else arousing fears of "neocolonialism" and thus a reaction against cooperation.

In the practical expression of these philosophies, the concepts of "community" and "participation" are basic. We saw in Chapter 2 how in most primitive societies all decisions were group decisions. The members of the tribe would talk and talk, everyone being allowed his say, until unanimous agreement was reached. In many countries this process of active participation was gradually crushed by feudal landlords and by local or foreign bureaucracies, and attitudes of passive obedience set in. Many of the leaders of the new countries are now trying to revive traditional community participation in a modern context. One aspect of this policy is the insistence that women should play an active part in the political process. Gandhi brought women into the forefront of the Indian independence movement. And the women seem anxious to emerge; the astonished instructors of literacy campaigns in the jungles of Africa and Asia have been besieged by women demanding to be taught to read and write. A second aspect is the use of the mass media, normally the village radio and the travelling cinema, to instruct the villagers in such matters as hygiene and agricultural methods, and to give them information about the wider world; and a third is the involvement of the peasants in the political process through elected councils at different levels.

Two countries in particular have pioneered in policies of integrated development on a national scale—India, whose huge population (585 million in 1972), ancient culture and profound poverty places it beside the other Asian giant, China; and Tanzania, one of the newest and poorest countries in the world, with a population, in 1972, of 14 million.

India's situation in 1947 differed from that of China in several ways. First, it had no comparable linguistic homogeneity; in modern India there are fifteen official language groups. Second, it had no tradition of political unity; throughout the three thousand years of its recorded history it was normally divided into a number of independent states, united only for short periods. Third, there were deep religious divisions, notably between the Hindu majority and the fifty million Moslems who remained in India after the creation of Pakistan. Fourth, its caste system constituted a rigid social structure of a kind unique in the world. Fifth, India was—and is—a country permeated by a religion of a profoundly metaphysical, otherworldly nature, whereas Chinese Confucianism was essentially an ethical code about behavior in this world. Finally, two centuries of British rule meant that India experienced the shock of the Western impact in a different way from China. British rule was psychologically humiliating; but it was based, in theory at least, on indoctrinating the Indians in the ideas of constitutional government, justice and personal rights which the British had themselves pioneered in the modern world. In contrast to China's Communist leaders, the men and women who led India's independence movement and founded modern India—Gandhi, Nehru, Radhakrishnan, Mrs. Gandhi, to name but a few—were students or professors in Britain, and were and are personalities of cosmopolitan experience. In 1947 India thus faced fundamental problems of divisiveness—linguistic, political, religous and social—as well as of development; but its assets were a spiritual tradition quite incompatible with the crude and aggressive dogmatism of Marxism, allied to a solid grounding in the positive humanist values of the West.

India's economic development is taking place within the framework of a democracy of the British type: a multiparty system functioning through a Federal Parliament and twenty-one state legislatures, and an executive vested in a prime minister who is the leader *inside* Parliament of the party or coalition of parties commanding a parliamentary majority. The five national elections held since 1947 have been free and fair, despite the general illiteracy of the electors. The multiparty legislative bodies at the federal and state levels are going concerns in which daily, and often acrimonious, debates take place. They are underpinned by elected multiparty bodies at the district, neighborhood and village levels called *panchayats*—as in China, each grade of council elects the one above it. India has always had village councils; but for the first time self-government at the district level replaces the autocracy of centuries. The intention is that through this hierarchy of indirectly elected councils power will be diffused from its present excessive concentration in the State and Federal governments, so that ultimately India will become a "communitarian society"—to use the phrase of the Gandhian statesman Jayaprakash Narayan—with its basis in a federation of villages.

The economic structure of the country is modeled on that of postwar Western Europe: a publicly and a privately owned sector, the whole operating within the framework of five-year plans. The public sector contains the major public utilities and heavy industries, steel and mining. A number of other key industries, such as aluminum, machine tools and fertilizers, are half publicly and half privately owned. The remaining industries are in private hands. Indian planning is more directive and less "indicative" than that of Western Europe; the

Indian Planning Commission, which is virtually independent of the Federal Parliament and State Legislatures, have no counterpart there. But the Commission has no enforcement powers, except in the small but vital sector of the economy directly controlled by the Government. The plans are drawn up in consultation with the state governments, which in turn discuss them with the regional *panchayats*—a process which may take about a year. The democratically structured political and planning processes are thus intermeshed.

The political and economic system is administered through what is almost certainly the best trained and most efficient civil service in the developing world—a British bequest. It includes not only a large corps of administrators selected by examination, but also experts in such subjects as taxation, public works, statistics and engineering—a vitally needed class of professionals which most of the poor countries lack.

The basic industrial infrastructure, started by the British, has now been established. India has, its planners say, achieved the first stage of an industrial revolution, resulting not only in an overall trebling of industrial production since the mid-fifties,[1] but in a great diversification of goods produced. India, like China, is now making machines of the most sophisticated kind, ranging from jet aircraft to computers. It has also launched itself into the atomic age, being the only poor country except for Pakistan to develop nuclear power for peaceful purposes. (Two reactors have been built and a third is being established.)

At first, as in China, higher priority was given to industry rather than to agriculture; but, as in China, this emphasis was soon reversed. Extensive land-reform legislation (land reform is a state, not a federal, matter) has eliminated the *zamindars,* with compensation, and laid down the principle of "land to the tiller." Ceilings on the size of holdings have been set, scattered plots are being consolidated, and tenants enabled to become owners. The "Green Revolution," inaugurated in the late fifties (see Chapter 17), means that crop yields can be revolutionized on small plots by "package inputs" of new kinds of seed, chemical fertilizers and water. (The pre-Green Revolution technology of mechanization requires large farms—tractors seed an area of at least twenty-five acres to yield an economic return[2]—and this intensifies rural unemployment.) A combination of small private holdings, cooperatives and Green Revolution technology thus seems to offer a viable alternative to the Chinese model as a way of modernizing agriculture while at the same time providing employment on the land. This is the Indian Government's basic policy; but its implementation is being impeded by the failure of the state legislatures, in which the landowners are an important political force, to carry out the land reforms fully. Meanwhile a rising class of landowning peasants is profiting from the Green Revolution to enter the market economy, and this is widening the gulf between the landowning class and the forty million who remain or are becoming landless laborers. It is significant, however, that when in 1959 Premier Nehru proposed the introduction of cooperative joint farming, involving the pooling of land and its centralized management—though the peasants would have retained their property rights and received ownership dividends—he encountered strong peasant resistance, and so did not pursue the idea. In the early seventies the Federal Government is putting great pressure on the state governments to implement the land-reform legislation.

The Federal Government's policy is to complement land reform by promoting agricultural efficiency and social justice through voluntary cooperatives and "community development." Cooperatives now exist in over 95 percent of the villages, and 45 percent of the argicultural population is covered. Their activities include the provision of agricultural credit (including Green Revolution seeds and fertilizers), marketing, processing and consumer trade.[3] An Indian professor, returning to his native Punjab from Canada in 1971, found the villages dotted with little government banks (for the banks have been nationalized), giving the peasant the cheap credit which frees him from the age-old grip of the money lender.[4] The annual turnover of the cooperatives, in the early seventies, was some two billion dollars.[5]

The cooperatives are complemented by a unique program of "community development," or "village uplift," based on a blending of the Gandhian ideal of *sarvodaya,* a classless society inspired by nonviolence and brotherly love, and Western ideas of "social engineering" and "group dynamics." The policy, launched in 1952, involves grouping the villages into Blocks of about sixty to one hundred, with a population of about seventy thousand, each supervised by a Block Development Officer and by the elected neighborhood *panchayat.* Each Block is divided into circles of five or six villages under the supervision of a Village Level Worker, *gram sevak,* or servant of the village community. His task is to stimulate the villagers, through the cooperatives and the village *panchayats,* to build schools, improve sanitation, pave and light their lanes (electricity now reaches one village in ten),[6] develop agriculture and minor industries and, by his presence and example, to inculcate new attitudes of mind. Funds are allocated by the Federal and state governments, and the villagers also contribute cash, materials and labor. By 1970 community development programs were in operation in most of the villages of India, and since they are part and parcel of the *panchayat* system, they are democratically controlled. The alliance of technology and social reform has begun to lift Indian agriculture off the ground. We shall see in Chapter 17 that standards of nutrition are still far too low, and that there is great scope for increased yields. But between 1951 and 1971 production of food grains doubled, from 55 million tons to over 100 million tons,[7] while population rose 64 percent, from 361 to 565 million. In bad years India, like China, has had to rely on imports of food grains (mainly from America) to avert famine, and a major extension of water storage and irrigation schemes is needed to end the age-long dependence on the vagaries of the monsoon. Nevertheless, it is significant that India was able to feed ten million refugees from Bangladesh for nine months.

The attempt to solve India's basic problems within the framework of political democracy and a mixed economy means that progress has been very uneven. The social problems of urbanization and unemployment, described in Chapter 6, have still to be seriously tackled. The development of intermediate technology has only just become a matter of government concern; an "Appropriate Technology Cell" has been established within the Ministry of Industry. The doubling of life expectancy from thirty-five years in 1950 to forty-seven in 1970 [8] is partly the result of the establishment of rural health clinics; but health services are still essentially structured in the Western model described in Chapter 8. The education system needs fundamental structural reform. The welfare state does not yet exist in India. The imaginative population-control measures which the government has been taking for two decades (see Chapter 5) have not brought the birthrate down to the level achieved in China, partly because of the lack of social security and of rural health services, and partly because the Indian masses, unlike those of China, are not being dragooned by their government into new behavior patterns in their personal lives. Dangerous inequalities in the level of incomes still exist. The Fourth Plan for 1969–74 states that: "Available information does not indicate any trend toward reduction in the concentration of income and wealth." [9]

Nevertheless, India's unique experiment in seeking to bring 585 million people into the modern world in the context of political democracy, a mixed economy and democratic planning has weathered its first 25 years. "A new breed of Indian is coming forward; healthier, better educated, more aware and demanding more than previous generations, and much more disposed to try something new." [10] India's economy and its society are on the move. This very movement is arousing the fears of all the sectional interests—linguistic, caste, religious, industrial and landowning; and at times these fears seem to be producing a state of anarchy to which an authoritarian regime of the Right or the Left would be the only solution. But if India muddles through, it may manage to deal with the problems which the Chinese are already solving, while simultaneously dealing with those problems which the Chinese have not yet faced—that is, it may manage to combine economic development and growth with social justice and personal and political freedom.

Tanzania's policies are based on *Ujamaa* or "familyhood," President Nyerere's formulation of African socialism. Its three basic principles are: "Mutual respect between members of the society, common property, and an obligation to work. The strategy then is to build on these principles of traditional society." [11]

The economic structure of the country is essentially socialist. In 1967 foreign banks, import-export and wholesale businesses were nationalized, and the government took a majority control in a number of important manufacturing enterprises. It also took over private schools and hospitals. Foreign investments were thus virtually eliminated. The government controls prices of cloth and basic foodstuffs. It therefore ensures that imports are limited to goods essential for development and welfare, and that luxuries are eliminated.[12]

Politically, *Ujamaa* is expressed in a somewhat unique system. The single party, the Tanganyika African National Union (TANU), allows its candidates to be elected by the people from lists of names produced in the towns and villages. In each constituency the Party choses two people from the list to run for Parliament. Since many voters are illiterate, each candidate has a symbol, such as a house or a hoe. For administrative purposes the country is divided into regions, each with councils elected at the regional, district and village level, and with development committees to participate in national planning. Elitism at the top is being broken by such measures as forbidding officials to hold shares in or directorships of companies and to receive rent from houses, curbing their salaries and pegging industrial wages. All energies are being concentrated on developing schools, agricultural and health services, rural water supplies and minor industries in the countryside, with popular participation. Examinations in school are being downgraded, and primary education is being developed as an end in itself, instead of as a lead-in to secondary education; all higher education students at home and abroad take courses which are geared to the Five-Year Plan, and are committed to serve the government for five years after graduation; and a voluntary corps of "National Service" pioneers is clearing the bush and starting new farming methods. Some fifteen hundred "*Ujamaa* villages" have been established. They are run on "communal" lines. Private plots are allowed, but each peasant has a task assigned him to perform for the community. The village officials are elected by the villagers at their general meetings, which may occur twice a week. Each village or group of villages runs its own affairs in its own way, evoking government help when it needs it.[13] A significant feature of these experiments is the development of UNESCO's ideas of functional literacy (see below) by the villagers themselves.

"Three hundred thousand Wagogo tribesmen have suddenly decided to abandon their ancient way of life in favor of the modern socialist communal system of agriculture," wrote a British journalist in 1971. So they turned up at the sites where eighty new villages were being built. No one was expecting them and the huts were not yet built. "Ten days ago President Nyerere left his capital for a camp in one of the new villages to take charge of an operation to settle the Wagogo. I found him making bricks with his hands in the traditional way and leading a team of his personal bodyguard and staff in competition with other teams made up of the country's top civil servants, police and army officers. . . ." He was spending eight and a half hours a day making bricks.[14]

In 1971 TANU issued its "Guidelines on Guarding, Consolidating and Advancing the Revolution of Tanzania, and of Africa." This document reflects a new tone of disillusionment with the West. The term "development" is now linked with "liberation"—of Southern Africa from white racist rule and of Black Africa from European "exploitation." The overthrow by military coups of other socialist leaders of Africa—President Obote of Uganda and President Keita of Mali—is attributed to the plotting of the imperialists. It was therefore decided, in the same year, to create a "Peoples' Militia" to combat these threats. At the same time, President Nyerere is increasingly emphasising Tanzania's determination to be "self-reliant." When independence was attained in 1961 the country possessed only one hundred African graduates out of a (then) population of ten million. Its development still depends upon an elite corps of university professors, experts and managers from the rich countries, as well as on foreign aid to finance 40 percent of the Second Development Plan. But the expatriates are being replaced as rapidly as possible by Tanzanians, and aid is accepted only if it does not have "strings" which compromise the government's political principles (see Chapter 14). Most of Tanzania's aid comes from China, which has given a twenty-five million-dollar interest-free loan.[15]

We shall suggest later in this book that the increasing interdependence of the rich and the poor countries is in the logic of events. Tanzania's present policies of "self-relience" in national integrated development is a sign to the West that the world community cannot develop as long as white racism is tolerated and aid is given in exploitative ways.

In general, the poor countries have adopted the economic model of Western Europe: a mixed economy, as in India, with a public, a private and sometimes an intermediate sector, combined with economic planning. Naturally the spectrum ranges widely, from economies based mainly on private enterprise, such as most of those of Latin America and many of those of Africa, to countries like Egypt, Syria, Sri Lanka, Burma, Algeria and Guinea, where most enterprises have been brought under state ownership.

By 1971 almost all the poor countries, even such remote medieval fastnesses as Bhutan and Nepal, had four- or five- or ten-year development plans—Brazil was a notable exception. Until the late sixties these plans were based on the assumption that the fundamental objective was growth. The planners thought (as European economists thought before 1939) that social hardship was an inevitable feature of the growth process, and that in due course a rising growth rate would automatically bring rising prosperity to all. Now they are adopting a new approach. They are beginning to think of social justice as an objective in its own right, and therefore to take into account the effects of GNP growth on the problems of mass poverty, and to give greater emphasis to social reforms. The Peruvian plan for the early seventies, for example, allots 50 percent of its public funds to agrarian reform and the resettlement of peasants on land expropriated under laws of 1969 and 1971–72.[16] (We shall see in Chapter 15 that this change of philosophy is reflected at the international level in the United Nations Second Development Decade Strategy for the Seventies.)

The plans suffer, in general, from a lack of dependable statistics—statistical services in the poor countries are generally rudimentary; of adequate budget-accounting systems and, above all, of good administrators. (Even in the rich countries the limitation on the implementation of economic plans is not financial resources, but administrative capacity.) As a result, there is a great gap between promise and performance; and in the mixed economies most growth increases are often in the private sector, and sometimes in forms inimical to the plan's provisions. This may be because Western investors, with their vast resources of technical and managerial skills, are partly making up for these local deficiencies. Another impediment to the plans is the political instability described in Chapter 9.[17]

The new importance attached to social policies affects not only the nature of the plans but the methods of implementing them. The idea, already well developed in India and Tanzania, that planning at the national level should be related to "community development" at the local level is spreading very rapidly—so much so that, according to a United Nations report, "action in most regions has outstripped theory." When national planning and community development started they were poles apart, but "a decade has sufficed" for it to be recognized that they must be interlocked—the plans will not be effective unless they are based on popular participation; and conversely, as Sri Lanka's Ten-Year Plan for the sixties pointed out, community development, "by mobilizing manpower on a voluntary or self-help basis for construction work, could release substantial financial resources for other uses." [18]

In those regions where large estates exist (see Chapter 6), land reform is a prerequisite for community development. The following experience illustrates what community development can achieve and shows how the absence of land reform can stand in its way. In 1952 Professor Allen R. Holmberg, an anthropologist at Cornell University in the United States, rented for five years the *hacienda* of Vicos, at an altitude of two miles above sea level on the plateau of central Peru. The initial attitude of the seventeen hundred serfs, over whom, as patron, he held absolute power, and whose ancestors had worked on the state since 1594, was extremely hostile. But it soon began to change. The professor learned Quechua, the Indian tongue of the peasants. He held weekly discussion meetings with them at which all were encouraged to speak up. He abolished the patron's rights to personal service, and declared the crops from the patron's land to be community property, to be sold in order to accumulate cash reserves with which the peasants could eventually buy the estate. He showed them how to grow better potatoes by modern methods, and encouraged them to market these potatoes in Lima and to use the proceeds to build a school and clinic. By the time his lease was up they had elected a council of ten to govern themselves. Finally, in 1962, with their savings they bought the estate from the government, which had bought it from the owner.

The experience was contagious. The government became enthusiastic and enlarged the Vicos school as a nucleus for a rural school system. Some local landlords cooperated by donating land for the new schools. Others reacted differently. When the serfs of Chancos, an adjoining estate, asked a group of government ministers who were visiting Vicos (an almost unheard of event) to extend the Vicos program to their estate, their master had them flogged. And when the Indians on Huapra, another adjoining estate, began constructing a new school building for their own children and cultivating uncultivated fields, the mas-

ter called in fifteen national policemen and shot the villagers down.[19] *
Planning at the national level is therefore a general and consistent
policy in the poor countries. But its complement, community development at the village level, is at present, in most countries other than
India and Tanzania, a patchy affair, bound up, except in Africa, with
the problem of land reform.

In most of the countries of Asia and the Middle East major land
reforms, involving the redistribution of land and the establishment of
cooperatives, have been enacted since 1945. In Latin America, by
1972, land reform had been carried out in Mexico, Bolivia and Cuba,
and had been set in motion in Chile and Peru. In the rest of the continent there have only been piecemeal measures, despite growing agi-
tation for fundamental change. In the Charter of Punte del Este of
1961, which gave expression to President Kennedy's "Alliance for Progress," the United States Government and the governments of all the
Latin American states except that of Cuba pledged themselves to promote reforms which would replace the *latifundia* and *minifundia* "by
a just system of property." But when it has come to the crunch the
United States Government, haunted by the behavior of Cuba, has
fought shy of specifically recommending radical expropriation and redistribution in Latin America. It has contented itself with supporting
the kind of policies which are being carried out in Venezuela and Colombia: the colonization of public lands and the govermental purchase
of relatively small areas, leaving the great estates virtually intact, and
adding to the *minifundia*. In Guatemala there has even been a backward movement. In the early fifties a left-wing regime nationalized
the land of the American-owned United Fruit Company and some of
the great landlords. In 1954 this regime was overthrown by a right-
wing dictator, with the covert help of the American Government,[20]
and the land was returned to the landlords and the company. Some
Latin American governments are evading land reform, with all its
knotty legal complications, by helping the richer farmers to increase
productivity through the Green Revolution.

The usual pattern of land reform in these three continents is similar to that which has been enacted in India. The Bolivian and Iranian
governments exempt large landowners from expropriation, provided
that they operate with large capital investment, produce cash crops
for sale, pay the workers in money and allow them to form unions.

The implementation of many of the land reforms in Asia has been
frustrated by the landlords—as in India. They have been really effec-

* Condensed and paraphrased by permission of *Saturday Review*.

tive only where the United States Government was able virtually to impose them at the end of World War II—in Japan, South Korea and Taiwan.[21] Nevertheless, the Chinese model seems to be as unpopular with peasants generally as it proved to be in India. In the late sixties the Tunisian Government, disregarding peasant feelings, nationalized and collectivized much of the land. Peasant riots immediately broke out, in which the women played a leading part. Animals were slaughtered to avoid confiscation. The government soon gave in and restored the major part of the land to private holdings, setting up "mutual aid organizations" to avoid the use of the unpopular word "cooperative," with its implications of Communist collectivism.[22]

Mexico, which carried out a socialist revolution over half a century ago, has developed a mixed agrarian system, with a public and a private sector. Half the agrarian labor force, working nearly 40 percent of the land, are settled in *ejidos,* rural communities in which the land belongs to the village but is farmed in individual plots which cannot be subdivided or sold.

In most parts of Africa the initial problem of agricultural modernization is to replace customary rights of tenure by modern systems of legal ownership, entrenched in modern codes of personal law—which may involve a change in fundamental social values. The trends lie in two directions: towards privately owned small holdings, producing for the cash economy—these are already well developed in certain countries, notably Kenya, Uganda, Nigeria and Ghana; and towards modernized forms of communal ownership, as in Tanzania.

It is generally recognized that cooperatives of the Western type are an essential adjunct to the private ownership of small plots, since they provide the services which enable the peasant who lacks capital, credit and technical knowledge to farm his plot efficiently, and thereby also eliminate the middlemen and money lenders. In some countries where land reform is being fairly effectively carried out, for example in Egypt, and in Peru since 1968, the formation of cooperatives is legally compulsory. We have seen that they are working fairly well in India. Elsewhere in Latin American and Asia, where land reform has not been effectively carried out, cooperatives cannot take much root. In sub-Sahara Africa, where there are no great landlords to dispossess, they have generally worked well, starting by marketing the cash crops, and going on to provide fertilizers, machinery and credit, and even helping to establish schools.[23]

In Asia and Latin America the combination of improved technology, especially Green Revolution technology, with halfhearted, ineffective land reform and the development of cooperatives, is producing explosive social tensions. A minority of enterprising peasants are profiting from the technology and the reforms, thus producing a new kulak class of peasant capitalists; but the rest are becoming even poorer because of the population explosion. The frustration of the dispossessed is expressed in peasant revolts and guerrilla movements.[24] Few of these countries have established comprehensive democratic structures like that of India through which the peasant electors *may* manage to secure real reforms. "Until the peasantry begins to vote in its own interests," said a World Bank land-reform expert at a Congress of Orientalists in 1971, "the chances are that integrated agrarian reforms in this part of the world by due process of law will be almost impossible." [25]

In other major aspects of integrated development—functional education, intermediate technology and community health services—new ideas are in the air, but implementation has been generally limited to small projects. The basic need in all three fields is to achieve a marriage between the traditional and the modern, for which the concept of "community development" within the context of national planning provides a framework. At present the average citizen of a poor country has the alternative of either remaining stuck in his traditional situation—which means remaining illiterate, using very primitive tools and having no health care—or else ineffectively imitating the West—gaining a Western-type education, trying to use sophisticated Western labor-saving machinery, perhaps supplied as "aid," and, if he is ill, getting (if he can) to a Western-type hospital.

In education the concept of the "community school" is being pioneered by UNESCO and other international bodies, and by a few leaders such as President Nyerere. Sir Hugh Springer, a distinguished educationist from Barbados, has written: "The concept of the community school as an instrument for the transformation of the whole community, involving children and parents alike, is more appropriate [than formal schooling of the Western type] to relatively isolated rural comunities engaged in modernizing their traditional agriculture. In such schools the curriculum will be based, not simply on imported books and materials, but on the local flora and fauna, the local customs and social organization; using the countryside as a laboratory and the life of the village as a case study." [26] UNESCO has launched a number of projects in "functional literacy," based on the realization that if the literacy of the child or the adult is to endure, "it must be clearly seen as a quite essential element . . . in 'development,' be it in the economic, social, cultural or political field." [27] In other words, the student must feel that his education is relevant to his real opportunities in a "developing" country.[28] The complement to the community school and to functional literacy is to bring the modern world into the villages, partly by sending students into the cities to study such subjects as argicultural technology, home economics and para-medicine, which they can then apply in the villages when they return, and partly through the mass media. We have already referred to the village radio and the travelling cinema. In the future the new Western technology—the computer and the radio and television pro-grams broadcast by satellite—could help to transform teaching and teacher-training, and, incidentally, to promote international coopera-tion, for in areas like West and East Africa and Central America such programs could be developed on a regional basis.[29] "I feel in my bones that we are on the edge of great educational changes (just as I believe that what future historians will judge to be an era of wholeness and integration has already begun)," said Sir Hugh Springer at a Common-wealth Conference on Human Ecology in 1970. "Things move fast nowadays, and the break-through may begin at any moment. Modern instruments and media of communication will provide the means for it." [30]

The development of community schooling and functional literacy for adults and children is bound up with the development of "inter-mediate technology," labor-intensive technology which is also a key factor in reducing unemployment. We have already noted the great emphasis which the Chinese are placing on it. In 1971 the United Nations Conference on Trade and Development (UNCTAD) held the first meeting of its Intergovernmental Group on the Transfer of Tech-nology (from the rich to the poor countries). A World Bank expert pointed out that the rich countries' concern, on which their research is concentrated, is with labor-saving technology for their own use. He found that they had no incentive to fashion intermediate tech-nology for the poor countries; that no great improvisations were going on in the poor countries themselves; and that no major research insti-tutions were devoting energies to it, "aside from a small group in Britain, operating on a shoe-string budget." [31] This group (The In-termediate Technology Development Group, Ltd., London) has al-ready inspired a number of small projects, such as the invention of a machine to grind cassava in their workshop in Zaria, Nigeria. This machine is made, locally, of bicycle parts, plywood, iron water pipe, and old hacksaw blades, and costs about $25. The previous alternatives for the Nigerian housewife were to grind by hand, or to buy a foreign machine costing about $5,000.

The same situation applies in the field of health. Although many countries have started to set up rural health clinics, nothing com-parable to the Chinese system of "barefoot doctors," linked to regional hospitals and bringing basic medical care to all citizens, has been developed, except in Cuba. Such clinics, staffed by medical auxiliaries (substitute doctors with lower professional qualifications than those demanded in the West) and paramedical personnel (nurses, pharmacists, laboratory technicians and health inspectors) are particularly suited to deal with the kind of diseases which occur in the poor countries (see Chapter 8). They can also provide family-planning, child-welfare and other preventive services. One health clinic case in a hundred has to be referred to a district hospital, and a district hospital in turn has to refer about 1 percent of its cases to a regional or national hospital for specialists' services. One health center may cost around $50,000—whereas at present a poor country may be spending $12,500 on one bed in a glossy new hospital and $75,000 on the training of one doctor to function in it. "Nigeria spends six times as much on curative medicine as it does on preventive; yet it has been estimated that even a doubling of the expenditure on preventive medicine would transform the whole medical picture there." [32]

The non-Communist poor countries are trying to solve their problems in terms of the ideas of "community" and "participation." In this they are confronted with at least three kinds of difficulty. The first is the opposition of the vested interests within their own borders—the landowning class, the business interests, the elites—to the structural changes needed. The second is the magnetic pull exercised by the West towards inappropriate models, institutions and technology, a pull which much Western aid and investment is reinforcing (see Chapter 14). Revolutionary upheavals may be required in order to achieve "liberation" for development. The third difficulty concerns motivation, or inspiration. The example of China shows how a simplistic and dogmatic ideology provides the dynamism for integrated development. Can the more spiritual, undogmatic, humanitarian and undefined philosophies of the non-Communist countries generate the same dynamism? We can only express our faith that they can. For the concepts of community, of universal brotherhood, of all men as children of God, ring more sweetly in the ears of the soul than do the doctrines of Marx and Mao. But if these philosophies are to prevail in the next crucial decades, the rich countries must play their part.

References

1. Ministry of Information and Broadcasting, Government of India, *India, A Reference Annual, 1970,* p. 327.

2. W. Klatt, "Agrarian Issues in Asia, I," in *International Affairs* (London: The Royal Institute of International Affairs), Vol. 48, No. 2, April 1972, p. 237.

3. *India, A Reference Annual, 1970, op. cit.,* p. 279.

4. Information given to the author by Dr. Darshan Sarih of Notre Dame University, British Columbia, Canada.

5. Information given to the author by the Advisor on Co-operatives to the Overseas Development Administration of the British Foreign Office.

6. Donald S. Connery, "India Defuses the Population Bomb," in *Vista, Journal of the United Nations Association of the United States,* November–December 1972, p. 50.

7. Patwant Singh, *The Struggle for Power in Asia* (London: Hutchinson and Co., 1971), p. 122.

8. *India, A Reference Annual,* 1973, p. 95.

9. Planning Commission, Government of India, *Fourth Five-Year Plan 1969–74,* p. 11.

10. Donald S. Connery, *op. cit.,* p. 50.

11. See Julius K. Nyerere, *Ujamaa, Essays on Socialism* (Dar es Salaam: Oxford University Press, 1968), and Jimoh Omo-Fadaka, "Tanzanian Way to Self-Reliance," in *The Ecologist* (Richmond, Surrey, England), February 1972, pp. 9–11.

12. Jimoh Omo-Fadaka, *op. cit.*

13. *Ibid.,* and J. Cameron and W. A. Dodd, *Society, Schools and Progress in Tanzania* (Oxford, England: The Pergamon Press, 1970).

14. *The Observer* (London), July 18, 1971.

15. Jimoh Omo-Fadaka, *op. cit.*

16. FAO: *State of Food and Agriculture, 1971* (Rome, 1971), pp. 79–80 and 92–93.

17. Albert Waterson (of the World Bank), *Development Planning: Lessons of Experience* (Baltimore, Md.: Johns Hopkins Press, 1965), pp. 198–99, 246, 289, 365–67.

18. United Nations, *Local Participation in Development Planning: A preliminary study of the relationship of community development to national planning* (New York: United Nations, 1967), pp. 3–4.

19. Henry F. Dobyns, et. al., "A Contagious Experiment," in *Saturday Review,* November 3, 1962, pp. 59–62 (condensed).

20. Eduardo Galeano, "With the Guerrillas in Guatemala," in *Latin America, Reform or Revolution?,* ed. James Petras and Maurice Seitlin (Greenwich, Conn.: Fawcett Publications, Inc., 1968), p. 376.

21. W. Klatt, *op. cit.,* p. 240.

22. Information given to the author by Sir Edward Warner, former British Ambassador in Tunisia.

23. Information given to the author by Mr. Donald Shepard of the Kennedy School of Government, Harvard University.

24. See W. Klatt, "Agrarian Issues in Asia, II," in *International Affairs* (London: The Royal Institute of International Affairs), Vol. 48, No. 3, July 1972.

25. *The New York Times,* January 13, 1971.

26. Sir Hugh Springer, "Development—Problems of Understanding," in *Chemistry in Britain,* Vol. 8 No. 12, December 1972, p. 516.

27. Harold Houghton, formerly Deputy Education Advisor to the British Colonial Office, in a letter to Sir Hugh Springer of January 1973.

28. See UNESCO, *Long-term Outline Plan for 1971–76* (Paris, 1970) and *Five Years After Teheran—World Literary Program* DDG/70/14 (September 1970) and Experimental World Literacy Program, ED-71/Conf. 43/4, July 1971.

29. UNESCO, *Communications in the Space Age* (Paris, 1968), p. 64.

30. Sir Hugh Springer, in an address given to the First Commonwealth Human Ecology Conference, Malta, October 1970.

31. Intermediate Technology Development Group, Ltd., London, *Annual Report 1970–71,* p. 6.

32. Intermediate Technology Development Group, Ltd., booklet, *Health, Manpower and the Medical Auxiliary)* (London: 1971).

twelve

TRADE RELATIONS BETWEEN THE RICH AND THE POOR COUNTRIES

Exports account for 80 percent of the poor countries' foreign-exchange earnings. These earnings rose generally in the sixties at a rate twice that of the later fifties; but they have not risen fast enough to keep up with development plans and needs.[1]

Ninety percent of the poor countries' export earnings derive from primary products—the unprocessed crops and minerals which in many cases the ruling colonial power first started to farm or mine. Nearly half of them earn more than 50 percent of their export receipts from a single commodity. Fuel exports account for a third of all their export earnings, but three-quarters of these fuel earnings, increasing at a rate of 10 percent a year, go to six countries containing less than 3 percent of the world's population.[2] Apart from fuel, exports of primary products have increased at half the rate of world trade in general, owing to a decline in world demand. The United States, for example, consumes some 40 percent of the world's imports of coffee, which is the largest single source of the poor countries' foreign-exchange earnings after petroleum; but the American demand has remained static since the early sixties. Imported cane sugar—the main export crop of Jamaica and other Caribbean islands—competes with the subsidized beet sugar produced in the rich countries of Western Europe. Other primary products, such as cotton, wool, jute and natural rubber, are being superseded by synthetic materials. Between 1954 and 1966 the consumption of cotton and wool increased by 10 percent, and of manmade fibers by 500 percent.[3]

This general fall in demand has resulted in a steady decline in the terms of trade of the poor countries. The prices of their exports to the rich countries have fallen drastically in relation to the prices of their imports from them, which rose by some 15 percent in the sixties.

To give but one example: "In 1960 one ton of Cameroon cocoa paid for 2,700 metres of imported cloth; in 1965, only 800 metres." [4]

Agreements have been made between exporting and importing countries to stabilize the prices of certain primary commodities—wheat, tin, olive oil, sugar, coffee and cocoa. These agreements, which the poor countries would like to see extended to many more commodities, have proved difficult to administer. The sugar agreement of 1969 was not signed by the United States, or by the European Community countries, which are in fact giving export subsidies to their exporters to dump their expensive beet sugar on foreign markets. [5]

To offset dependence on unstable world markets for primary products, the poor countries are trying to diversify their exports, mainly by developing processed primary products, such as canned foods and cotton textiles and other relatively unsophisticated manufactured goods. They are therefore directing to the rich countries two-thirds of their exports of manufactured goods. But eighty poor countries together supply only 5 percent of the world's total exports of manufactured and semimanufactured goods; and half of this 5 percent comes from only five countries—Hong Kong, India, Yugoslavia, Mexico and Taiwan. [6] Furthermore, a vicious circle is involved in this policy, since in order to expand their manufactures the poor countries may need to import—and pay for—additional capital equipment.

The poor countries' exports to the rich countries are also impeded by the latters' protective policies. The most common protective devices are tariffs (taxes on imports), quotas (limitations on the quantity of a particular import), subsidies (government grants to home producers or exporters) and, increasingly, national health, safety and environmental regulations. We noted in Chapter 3 that since 1945 the rich countries have liberalized their trade with each other, mainly through tariff reductions, negotiated through the General Agreement on Tariffs and Trade (GATT). This organization, established in 1948 after the United States Senate had prevented the setting up of an International Trade Organization, is simply a treaty conferring recognized rights and obligations on its contracting parties, which consist of some eighty rich and poor countries. It organizes country-to-country bargaining to make reciprocal tariff cuts, and thereby regulates about 80 percent of world trade. The United States took the lead in the great process of removing tariffs in six long "rounds" of GATT negotiations, culminating in 1967. When these cuts are finally implemented the average level of the American tariff will have been reduced from 50 percent in 1930, to 9 percent. [7] But GATT reductions apply essentially to manufactured goods. Almost all the rich countries are determined to "protect" their farmers by tariffs on agricultural goods—agricultural protectionism has increased since 1945, the worst offender being the European Community—which are all that many poor countries have to offer for export. Moreover, the principles of reciprocity and nondiscrimination on which GATT is based are largely meaningless for poor countries, which have little to offer at the bargaining table. In 1961 the representative of Pakistan at GATT said, "It is like asking a person who has no income to produce evidence of his earnings if he wants to earn more." [8] Robert McNamara said in 1972 that "the levels of tariffs on imports of manufactured goods from rich and poor trading partners respectively average out in the United States to 7 and 12 percent, in the United Kingdom to 9 and 14 percent, and in the European Community to 7 and 9 percent." [9] The poor countries, which make up two-thirds of the members of GATT, thus tend to regard it as a club for the rich.

Frustration at the general failure of the rich countries to help them to improve the terms of their trade led the poor countries to press for the establishment in 1964 of the United Nations Conference on Trade and Development (UNCTAD). The task of this body, which has no executive powers and can only make recommendations to governments, is to relate trade and aid to economic development in the poor countries. All the poor countries, including China, belong to it. UNCTAD confronts GATT as "the poor man's pressure group."

Under the inspiration of the Argentinian economist Dr. Raoul Prebisch, its architect and first Secretary-General, UNCTAD has launched a new approach to the structure of world trade. Since 1945 Western economists have asserted that the best way to help the expansion of the poor countries' trade is simply to promote world-wide trade liberalization. But the theory of the nineteenth-century British economist David Ricardo of "comparative advantage"—that each country should specialize in what it can produce relatively cheaply—has also been brought into modern development theory by the assertion that each country should specialize in producing the goods which use more of its abundant—and, by implication, cheap—factors of production. The poor countries should, therefore, produce goods which can be made by labor-intensive methods, while the rich countries should concentrate on capital-intensive goods. Dr. Prebisch has argued, however, that the only way in which the rich countries can help the poor, whose "comparative advantage" is in goods for which the world demand is static or declining, is by positive policies of trade discrimination in their favor.[10] "To this end, he proposed that they should be allowed to adopt rational protective policies in their own markets, without retaliation by the developed countries; and that the latter should additionally grant (preferential) access in their markets to the products of the developing countries. These concessions, he argued, would not only produce a more realistic reciprocity in trade relations; they were necessary to fashion a trade policy for development in conformity with the objective and obligations of the United Nations' Development Decade" [11] (see Chapter 15). UNCTAD has thus called on the rich countries to launch a planned restructuring of world trade to help the poor countries onto their feet. In 1967, a Summit Conference of representatives of seventy-seven poor countries issued the "Charter of Algiers," affirming their demand for these new policies; this was reinforced at a further conference of the poor countries, whose numbers had swollen to ninety-six, held at Lima in October 1971.

The starting point is the Generalized Preference Scheme, under which *all* the rich countries should give tariff preferences to imports from *all* the poor countries. Agreement was reached in 1970 between the rich members of UNCTAD (including the Soviet bloc) and ninety-one poor countries to introduce the scheme for a period of ten years for most manufactured and semimanufactured goods—excluding processed foods, a type of export which the poor countries are particularly anxious to develop. They were not, however, able to agree on a common scheme; each rich country or group of rich countries is introducing its own. By September 1973 those of the European Community (including Britain), the Nordic countries and Japan were in force, but the United States Congress had not yet enacted the American scheme. The European Community has only agreed to apply the scheme within the framework of existing quotas—and quotas are now in general a greater barrier to trade than tariffs—and the United States Government has refused to include footwear and textiles, the most competitive of the manufactured goods which the poor countries export, accounting, in cost, for about a third of the total exports. The scheme is expected, in practice, to benefit only a few poor countries whose industrial sector is relatively developed— Hong Kong, South Korea, Singapore, Mexico and India.

The scheme may, nevertheless, represent the first move towards a deliberate rationalization and reorganization of the structure of international trade and the international division of labor. The poor countries would concentrate on exporting to the rich foodstuffs and minerals and the simpler manufactured goods of the type produced in the first industrial revolution by labor-intensive methods, and the rich on exporting the more sophisticated mechanisms of the second industrial revolution—though the rich countries also have a vast potential market in the poor countries for intermediate technology and cheap consumer goods. It has been estimated that if the Prebisch policy were fully applied, consumers and taxpayers in the rich countries could be saved some twenty to thirty billion dollars at present spent on agricultural subsidies and artificially high food prices; and that they could also reduce the cost of the manufactured goods which they consume by fifty billion dollars by opening their doors fully to imports of such goods from the poor countries.[12] The increase in purchasing power which the poor countries would gain would enable the rich countries to expand their exports to them on a massive scale. Within the rich countries the money saved could be used to provide "adjustment assistance"—government aid to industry and agriculture to be used to adjust to the new patterns of world trade.[13] "It is a political fact of life that the developed countries must adopt realistic adjustment policies to cushion the impact of import competition by retraining, relocation, and refinancing. Few have done so to date. Until they do, labor and management opposition to trade liberalization will be great—and justly so," said Mr. McNamara at the Third UNCTAD Conference in 1972.[14]

The growing realization that the present international trading system, as represented by GATT, operates unfairly towards the poor countries, may therefore provide the impetus towards the creation of a world trade community. The need for adjustment policies within the rich countries will require more systematic internal planning (see Chapter 3). The need to meet the real development requirements of the poor countries will require trade policies geared to their development plans, which will thereby be prodded into realistic life. And the overall need to give the poor countries a fair deal within the international trading system, and to promote their development through it, may prompt the revival of the plan for a World Trade Organization, with effective planning and executive powers.

We shall return to the subject of trade, with particular reference to the Third UNCTAD Conference of 1972, in Chapter 15.

References

1. Lester B. Pearson (Chairman), *Partners in Development, Report of the Commission on International Development to the World Bank* (London: Pall Mall Press, Ltd., 1969), p. 70.
2. Robert S. McNamara, President of the World Bank, *Address to the United Nations Conference on Trade and Development*, Santiago, Chile, April 14, 1972. (Washington, D.C.: World Bank Pamphlet), p. 11.
3. Isaiah Frank, "International Trade Policy for the Second Development Decade," in *The International Journal of the Canadian Institute for International Affairs*, Vol. 25, No. 1, Winter 1969–70, pp. 97–98.

4. David Millwood (of the UNCTAD Secretariat), *Help or Hindrance? Aid, Trade and the Rich Nations' Responsibility to the Third World* (Geneva, Switzerland: Sodepax Pamphlet, 1971), p. 14.

5. "The future depends on the adjustment of agricultural markets," a discussion between experts in *Ceres, FAO Review*, Vol. 5, No. 2, March–April 1972, p. 40.

6. David Millwood, *op. cit.*, p. 12.

7. Joseph A. Greenwald, "The aims of the United States trade policy," in *Ceres, op. cit.*, p. 44.

8. David Millwood, *op. cit.*, p. 17.

9. Robert S. McNamara, *op. cit.*, p. 13.

10. I am indebted for this point to Mr. Peter Tulloch of the Overseas Development Institute, London.

11. Antony Tasker, *UNCTAD and the Commonwealth*, Henry Morley Lecture, Overseas Development Institute, London, 1970. (Reprinted from the Journal of the Royal Society of Arts, March 1970), pp. 213–14.

12. David Millwood, *op. cit.*, p. 20.

13. Caroline Miles, "Preference Systems: A Limited Achievement," in *Ceres, op. cit.*, p. 28.

14. Robert S. McNamara, *op. cit.*, p. 15.

thirteen

PRIVATE INVESTMENT
BY THE RICH COUNTRIES
IN THE POOR COUNTRIES

Capital is in short supply throughout the developing world. At present the poor countries finance 85 percent of their investment from their own savings. But, according to a United Nations expert panel, "the internal rate of capital formation in the developing countries is far below that necessary in order to promote a reasonable rate of per capita economic growth." [1] The problem is accentuated by the fact that two-thirds of the poor countries' investment must be devoted to the needs of the extra people who will be born—in the rich countries the proportion is one-quarter.[2] The experience of the Soviet Union and China shows that a poor country with great natural resources and huge reserves of labor can, through heroic effort and imposed discipline, generate its own development capital. (The initial impetus to both Russia's and China's industrialization was, however, provided by foreign capital before their Communist revolutions took place.) But most of the poor countries do not possess such rich and diversified resources; and perhaps they are not prepared—and should not be expected—to pay the heavy social costs of developing without external investment. The only alternative to forcing miserably poor peasants to save is, therefore, for the rich countries to provide the extra capital needed. This investment involves not only money but the transfer of vital technology.

The total private investment by the rich countries in the poor countries was estimated to have amounted in 1966 to some thirty billion dollars: 40 percent in petroleum; 9 percent in mining; 27 percent in manufacturing; and 24 percent in services, ranging from railways to hotels.[3]

A foreign investment produces a double flow of funds: out of the country in the form of profits to the shareholders in the rich countries, and into the poor country in the form of royalties (a share in the profits), taxes and wages to local employees. In a private-enterprise system the company will obviously want to gain an overall return on its total expenses, both capital and current. The system will impel it to try ultimately to take out of the country more than it has put into it. Estimates place the average rate of net return to investors in the rich countries at 8 to 14 percent.[4] The investment yield for the 7 great oil companies of the Western world fell from 14 percent in 1959 to 11.3 percent in 1969.[5] These rates are sufficiently attractive to stimulate a steady increase in the flow of private investment into the poor countries—the annual total rose from $3.1 billion in 1961 to $8.2 billion in 1971.[6] A French expert has estimated the net annual flow of money *from* Latin America and Asia to the United States at $1.5 billion a year.[7]

The primary concern of the companies of the rich countries in investing in the poor countries has not therefore been to help these countries to develop, but to extract goods for their own markets and profits for their shareholders. The overwhelming majority of their investment has been concerned with the production of raw materials for export, and their operations were in many cases started in the colonial period. In the past two decades many of these companies have tried hard to eliminate the taint of "imperialism" by such policies as employing as much local labor as possible, providing good amenities, paying good wages and permitting trade unions. The poor countries, for their part, are becoming increasingly self-confident and tough in negotiating with the foreign companies whenever they have had a good hand to play, as in the case of oil. The great oil companies of the rich world were astonished when, in 1970–71, abandoning the usual practice whereby each oil-producing country bargained on its own with the companies concerned, these countries—Venezuela, Nigeria, Indonesia, Libya, Iran, Iraq and the Persian Gulf States—acted as a group, the Organization of Petroleum Exporting Countries (OPEC), in a round of negotiations which produced a dramatic rise of oil revenues for them—the oil revenues of the Middle Eastern countries and Libya were expected to rise from $4.2 billion in 1970 to $10 billion in 1975,[8] nearly twice the total level of official "aid" to all the poor countries. The Middle East War of October 1973, however, has thrown the whole situation of Arab oil exports into extreme uncertainty.

Deep-rooted feelings of fear and hostility center, however, around foreign investment, particularly since few, if any, other poor countries have an asset comparable to oil with which to bargain. First, there is the straightforward fear of imperialist bullying. "I recall a spokesman of a major United States company boasting . . . to a group of newsmen . . . that his company had prevented the installation of a single new telephone in a major Latin American capital city for ten years until the government of that country had agreed to the company's terms for a new agreement," writes an American journalist.[9] Second, the poor countries fear that in a world of shrinking resources, the rich countries may be tempted to use their private investments as a means of establishing a politico-military stranglehold over them to ensure their own supplies of strategic commodities such as oil. As President Nyerere of Tanzania put it: "Small nations are like indecently dressed women. They tempt the evil-minded." Third, the social reformers in the poor countries see the links with foreign private enterprise as bolstering up their own elite class. Fanned by foreign advertising, these elites are encouraged to import luxuries, or goods of low development priority. The American sociologist Oscar Lewis, in a painfully moving account of a Mexican nouveau riche middle-class family, describes how they are determined that their clothes, cars and household goods shall be American, not Mexican, products.[10] Thus the efforts of the planners to gear their economies to production priorities are frustrated. (In Tanzania, to prevent this development, foreign enterprises operate in partnership with the state.) Fourth, the poor countries are worried by the fact that private foreign investment is the main channel for the import of technological know-how into their countries, a situation which a leading Latin American economist has described as "technological colonialism." [11]

Probably the greatest problem which foreign investment presents to the poor countries lies, however, in the power of the mighty multinational corporations from which most of it comes. These corporations are expanding at a rate of 10 percent a year—twice the rate of the world gross product.[12] The value of the industrial production outside their own countries of 150 companies, more than half of them American, was estimated for 1970 at over $450 billion—as compared with a total world trade figure of about $300 billion.[13] The assets of a single multinational corporation are therefore often greater than the GNP of several poor countries combined. It has been estimated that on the basis of present trends, by the year 2000 more than half the world's economy will be internationalized through these corporations.

A multinational company operates from a single point which, like the brain of an octopus, controls its subsidiaries all over the world. Its structure makes it a peculiarly effective medium for exporting technology and managerial skills, as well as for providing capital. It markets a wide variety of goods. It can switch production smoothly from one country to another, and from one commodity to another, as circumstances dictate. It stimulates the internationalization of services, such as banks and advertising, and even imposes a life-style, which has been called "cocacolonization." It helps to provide employment by setting up subsidiaries where labor is cheap—for example, American firms are producing textiles, foodstuffs and electronic goods in Taiwan, South Korea, Hong Kong and Mexico.[14] But the governments of many of the poor countries (and some of the rich) are increasingly worried by their inability to control this slippery international monster which is acquiring such a commanding position in their economies. The international economist Arthur Brown, a native of Jamaica, has said that many people in the poor countries would prefer to do without "aid" (in the sense of private investment—see Chapter 15) than be in the grip of these corporations.[15]

The general result of these fears is that most leftist regimes in the poor countries have expropriated the major raw material-producing foreign enterprises in their countries, especially those concerned with minerals and oil—Egypt, Burma, Sri Lanka, Chile, Mexico, Peru, Algeria and Zambia are a few examples. Usually they have paid compensation. But a great many companies, in particular those producing manufactured goods, have *not* been expropriated, and the OECD has suggested that the risks of expropriation are being exaggerated.[16] The Indian Government, for example, nationalized Indian-owned banks in 1970, but not those owned by foreign companies. Many countries are, however, practicing "creeping expropriation," subjecting foreign companies to heavy taxation, bureaucratic delays, impediments to the remission of profits and so on.

The tendency to expropriate means that the rich countries have a strong motive for disliking the leftist regimes, which advocate social justice, and for supporting conservative regimes, based on social privilege, which tend to be those which encourage foreign private enterprise. The rich countries are probably not motivated by the calculated malevolence which is sometimes attributed to them. More often their attitudes would seem to be ambivalent, since they also wish to foster in the developing world the principles of social justice which they are establishing at home. This is, for instance, one of the main objectives of the United States' Alliance for Progress with Latin America (see Chapter 15). But their attempts to undermine or overthrow regimes whose economic policies they dislike have been sufficiently frequent to cancel out much of the goodwill generated by their support of social reform.

The rich countries are beginning to realize that they will have to come to terms with the phenomenon of nationalization. One step in this direction is the provision of government insurance against the risks of expropriation, as well as of war; and an international investment insurance program is being considered.[17]

The problem of relating foreign private investment to development needs has now been espoused by the United Nations. Resolutions of 1968 by the United Nations Economic and Social Council and by UNCTAD enjoined the Secretary-General to work out "guidelines" for both rich and poor countries—a sort of international code of conduct. These would be complemented within the poor countries by guidelines for investment by foreign firms within the framework of development plans.[18]

The problem is, therefore, to ensure that foreign investment in the poor countries is geared to their real needs, while at the same time providing adequate safeguards and reasonable returns for the rich investors. Nationalization may not be an effective solution: the very word implies a step back to the limited assets of the nation-state, and away from the real advantages of the international services which the multinationals can provide. Increasing thought is being given to the possibility of bringing the multinationals under some form of international control. One aspect of this would be the creation of an international private-company law—at present national company law is being applied to what are in effect international bodies.[19] Another possible development is the organization of the international trade-union movement to cope with the monsters.[20] Rules for supervision by the United Nations are being considered by the Economic and Social Council of the United Nations.[21] A British Labor Party peer believes that "the best grouping to which Britain might look, as a means of restoring democratic control over production, distribution and exchange in the age of international capital, would be the enlarged European Economic Community." "In taking charge of incoming investment the EEC could also find ways of disciplining those international companies, which are based in Western Europe, in their behavior towards the developing countries."[22] Thus the "community" of rich countries which have pioneered in indicative planning, moderate socialism and the creation of the welfare state might pioneer in channeling the activities of the multinationals into the promotion of social justice in the poor countries. This would mean a far greater concentration on projects for social welfare and self-help; the development of capital and consumer goods for local consumption; of local manufactures to replace primary products for export; and the promotion of intermediate technology.

A significant pointer to the future, however, is the International Finance Corporation, established in 1956 as the private enterprise arm of the World Bank. "IFC is quite different from a multinational corporation. It is, so to speak, owned by its 95 shareholders, and so it owes its existence and its loyalty impartially to them all. It has no political objectives and it represents no special interests." [23] It thus combines multinational ownership with multinational activity—and the word "discipline" becomes unnecessary.

References

1. *United Nations Panel on Foreign Investment in the Developing Countries,* Amsterdam, February 1969 (U.N. Document E/4654/ST/ECA/117.), p. 4.

2. Angelos Angelopoulos, "Who aid whom?", in *Ceres, FAO Review,* No. 24, Nov.–Dec. 1971, p. 45.

3. Lester B. Pearson (Chairman), *Partners in Development, Report of the Commission on International Development to the World Bank* (London: Pall Mall Press, 1969), p. 100.

4. David Millwood (of the UNCTAD Secretariat), *Help or Hindrance? Aid, Trade and the Rich Countries' Responsibility to the Third World* (Geneva, Switzerland: Sodepax, 1971), pp. 29–30.

5. Theodore H. Moran, "The Problems of Oil: Coups and Costs," in *Foreign Policy* (New York, N.Y.: National Affairs Inc.), Fall, 1972.

6. OECD figures.

7. Claude Julien, *Les Trois Revolutions du Developpment* (Paris: Les Editions Ouvriers, 1968).

8. Charles Issawi, *Oil, the Middle East and the World* (Washington, D.C.: The Center for Strategic and International Studies, Georgetown University, 1972), p. 39.

9. Gary McEoin, *Latin America: The Eleventh Hour* (New York: P. J. Kenedy and Sons, 1962), p. 123.

10. Oscar Lewis, *Five Families* (New York: Basic Books, Inc., 1959).

11. Victor L. Urquidi, *The Challenge of Development in Latin America* (London: Pall Mall Press, Ltd., 1964), pp. 106–7.

12. Christopher Tugendhat, *The Multinationals* (London: Eyre and Spottiswoode, 1971), p. 3.

13. Albrecht Dueren, "Multinational companies as a political problem," in *The World Today,* Vol. 28, No. 11, November 1972 (London: The Royal Institute of International Affairs), p. 474n.

14. Roy A. Matthews, "The Multinational Corporation and the World of Tomorrow," in *Behind the Headlines,* Vol. 29, Nos. 3–4, Canadian Institute of International Affairs, May 1970, p. 14.

15. At a Conference on the United Nations Second Development Decade held by the United Nations Association of the United States in Boston on May 27, 1971.

16. "Foreign Investment in Developing Countries," in *OECD Observer,* No. 47, August 1970.

17. Rudolph S. Peterson (Chairman), *United States Foreign Assistance in the 1970's: A New American Approach.* Report to the President from the Task Force on International Development, March 4, 1970 (Washington, D.C.), p. 20.

18. Resolution No. 1359 of the Economic and Social Council of the United Nations of August 2, 1968, and Resolution No. 33(11) of UNCTAD of March 28, 1968.

19. Albrecht Dueren, in *op. cit.,* pp. 474–75.

20. *Ibid.,* pp. 479–81.

21. C. L. Sulzberger, in *The New York Times,* September 22, 1973.

22. Wayland Kennet, *Sovereignty and Multinational Companies,* Fabian Tract No. 409 (London: The Fabian Society, 1971), p. 4.

23. William S. Gaud, Executive Vice-President, International Finance Corporation, in a speech made on February 24, 1971.

fourteen

"AID" RELATIONS BETWEEN THE RICH AND THE POOR COUNTRIES

We have seen that private foreign investment and trade are not in general providing sufficient foreign currency to enable the poor countries to buy the capital equipment which they need to reach what the Pearson Report (a key report on international development made to the World Bank in 1969) has called the "take-off point" into "self-sustaining growth." The aim of aid is to bridge this gap.

The term "aid" is often used ambiguously. It implies some form of gift or charity, in contrast to private investment, which is expected to produce profits. The first great "aid" operation, the twelve-billion-dollars Marshall Plan, provided by the United States Government between 1948 and 1952 for the rebuilding of the war-shattered economies of Europe, was in fact a gift. But since the early sixties "aid" has become an official term, designating governmental and private flows from the rich to the poor countries. When an American or British company invests in another rich country, the operation is not regarded as aid; but when the company invests in a poor country, it is. We shall therefore use the word "aid" in its euphemistic sense, to include private investment; and the component of aid which is provided by the taxpayer, whether as government loans on "soft" terms, or as grants, "technical assistance" or contributions to international bodies, we will call governmental aid.

The idea that countries should aid each others' economic and social development is new in history. In 1949 President Truman followed up the outstandingly successful Marshall Plan by turning the attention of the American people, and the world, to the needs of the developing countries. He asked Congress for a grant of $45 million to aid them with technical assistance and capital investment. The United Nations responded by setting up a Technical Assistance Board within its Secretariat. As decolonization proceeded, the concept of aid gathered momentum. The decolonizing powers offered aid to their former colonies, partly to retain political influence, and partly, perhaps, as a sort of conscience money. By 1961 the total amount of governmental aid had risen from an average of $1.9 billion a year during 1950–55, to $5.2 billion. Private investment had risen from $1.6 billion a year to $3.1 billion.[1]

In 1961, at the suggestion of President Kennedy, the General Assembly of the United Nations pronounced the sixties the "Development Decade." It set two targets: an annual rate of economic growth of 5 percent of national income to be achieved by the developing countries, and a contribution by the rich countries of 1 percent a year of their national income in aid. (In 1968, at UNCTAD, the developing countries got this target raised by 25 percent by substituting GNP for national income. GNP takes no account of the costs of capital replacement, while national income is net of depreciation.)

Aid is given through two channels: by direct transfers from individual rich countries to individual poor countries (bilateral aid); and by international bodies—the United Nations, the Specialized Agencies, the World Bank and regional bodies like the Inter-American Development Bank and the European Community (multilateral aid). Less than 10 percent of the total amount given has been bilateral, though in 1971 the proportion had risen to 16 percent.[2]

Bilateral and multilateral aid take two main forms: the provision of capital and the provision of "technical assistance"—expert advisers to poor countries, expert training for their citizens and the carrying out of surveys and research. This technical assistance is the vital corollary to the capital development programs. All the multilateral and much of the bilateral capital aid is—unlike the Marshall Plan aid—given in the form of loans. The proportion of bilateral loans to grants rose from 13 percent in 1958 to 35 percent in 1968.[3] (Some of these loans are, however, on "soft" terms, with low interest rates and long repayment dates.) "Since the mid-1950's, publicly guaranteed debt (of the poor countries) has been growing at about 14 percent a year. At the end of 1971 it stood at over $60 billion and annual debt service exceeded $5 billion. Servicing of debt since the mid-1950's has been growing at the same average annual rate of about 14 percent. This is about twice the rate at which the export earnings, from which the debt must be serviced, have been growing. Such a relationship cannot continue indefinitely," said Mr. McNamara in 1972.[4] The poor countries are returning to the rich countries almost as much in debt services as they are receiving in official "aid" (see below).

Bilateral governmental aid is naturally conditioned by the interests of the donor country. Much of it has "strings" attached to it—Swedish aid is a notable exception. The main economic string is to "tie" it to purchases in the donor country. The donor thereby gets rid of surplus export goods and receives publicity in the recipient country. Although some recipients of American aid, for example, might prefer to purchase goods, such as vehicles, in Japan or Europe with their dollars, the conditions of aid prohibit this. By 1967, 84 percent of official aid was "tied"; this was estimated to reduce its real value by at least 20 percent.[5]

Then there are political strings. In the Act for International Development of 1961, Congress committed the United States Government to five principles in the allocation of aid: (i) "to strengthen the economies of underdeveloped friendly nations"; (ii) "to encourage the flow of private investment capital"; (iii) to promote, for those aided, an environment "free of pressures and erosion by the adversaries of freedom"; (iv) "to serve as an instrument of the Cold War" and (v) "to stimulate the growth and favor the equilibrium of the economy of the United States." The Charter of the Alliance for Progress of 1961, under which the United States offered to give Latin America (excluding Cuba) twenty billion dollars in aid over ten years, added a further criterion: the recipient countries are "to improve and strengthen democratic institutions"—which could be interpreted as arrogating to the donor country the right to sit in judgment on the political systems of the recipient countries.

The British and French simply give most of their bilateral aid to the countries which they formerly ruled. Ninety percent of British aid goes to the developing Commonwealth countries (with a total population of nine hundred million) and two-thirds of the French aid to the French-speaking countries of Africa (with a total population of eighty million).

The general result is a wide variation in the incidence of aid. In 1968, 90 percent of nearly four and a half billion dollars of American aid was given to fifteen countries, of which South Vietnam received four hundred million dollars and India three hundred million.[6] Overall bilateral aid in 1967–69 ranged from twenty-five dollars a head a year to Jordan, to three dollars a head a year to Indonesia.[7] Very high amounts were received by the ex-French North Africa and by South Korea and Taiwan, countries of great strategic importance to the United States; they are both aid success stories.

Just as an individual is free to give alms to whom he likes and in the way he wants, so the donor countries are naturally free to give their aid as and to whom they wish. But from the point of view of the needs of the developing world, this patchy pattern does not make sense. Inside the rich countries private charity, based on private likes and dislikes, is now a marginal activity. The real task of relieving want on a fair, comprehensive and dispassionate basis is entrusted to the welfare state.

The 16 non-Communist donor countries recognize that to give aid in the form of some 1,200 bilateral arrangements is not a very satisfactory situation. Various bodies for coordinating bilateral aid have therefore been set up. Some of these, such as the Colombo Plan Organization for aid to Southeast Asia and the Alliance for Progress for administering American aid to Latin America, involve both donors and recipients. The main forum where the donors coordinate their bilateral aid plans with each other is the Development Assistance Committee (DAC) of the OECD.

The multilateral aid given by the European Community to its eighteen Associated States in Africa is administered through institutions where donors and recipients meet as partners. The quantity of this aid is, however, very small—some hundred million dollars a year up to 1971 (it will be increased to nearly two hundred million dollars a year for the period 1971–75)—only a twentieth of the bilateral governmental aid supplied by the Community countries.

The multilateral aid of the United Nations and its affiliated Agencies is in theory coordinated through the United Nations Development Program (UNDP), described in the recent Jackson Report as a "non-system." "The machine as a whole has become unmanageable in the strictest sense of the word. As a result, it is becoming slower and more unwieldy, like some prehistoric monster." [8] The UNCTAD provides the only forum for coordinating bilateral and multilateral aid between all donors and all recipients, but it is not, strictly speaking, concerned with aid as such.

The general effect of all this coordinating machinery is limited. No authority is responsible for ensuring that targets of achievements are implemented. The nation-states, both donors and recipients, remain in sovereign self-control.

The programs of governmental and commercial aid are supplemented by the operations of private organizations—some of which have been working in the poor countries for a century. One of the most significant changes in the climate of thought in the past twenty-five years has been the new emphasis which all the religions of the world are giving to social service as a spiritual activity. Missionaries and voluntary workers in charitable organizations are often able to give an extra dimension to aid. Much heartache, for instance, may be caused by the sensible requirement of the UNDP that its experts should work in partnership with those of the countries which are being aided. The Tunisian agronomist, and the American agronomist who is showing him the latest know-how about the use of fertilizers, pesticides, new seeds and so on, spend their working day together. But the Tunisian's salary is a fraction of that of his American colleague. The latter goes home in the evening, in his large car, to a smart prestige house, while the former takes a bus to his modest apartment—to which he feels ashamed to invite the American. The missionaries and voluntary workers who live and work *with* the people as well as *for* them, irradiate the aid situation with human warmth.

In 1958 the British Government decided to add this extra dimension to official aid. It founded the Voluntary Service Overseas (VSO) in which young people enlisted for one or two years to work in the developing countries for subsistence pay. In 1961 President Kennedy established the United States Peace Corps on the same model, and Canada and other European countries followed suit. In 1970 the United Nations set up its own volunteer corps.

The young volunteers established an important image: that of the white man—and woman—gladly doing manual labor and living *with* the local people. This has helped to bridge the gulf inside the poor countries between the masses and their elites, who, with notable exceptions like President Nyerere of Tanzania, regard manual labor as the penance of the colored and the underprivileged. In the seventies unskilled volunteers are giving place to skilled specialists, since most of the poor countries now have their own agents of change, and find it insulting to be dependent upon unskilled foreigners to set an example.

The Communist countries' aid to the poor countries (including that of China, a poor country itself) has amounted to only about a twentieth of the aid given by the OECD countries—an estimated total of $12.2 billion between 1954 and 1970, of which the Chinese component was under $1 billion. Chinese loans are interest free; the Russians charge 2½ percent. The Russians have also trained some 10,000 students a year from the poor countries and sent an equivalent number of Soviet experts to these countries. This Communist aid, like that of the Western powers, is an adjunct of their political policies: by 1972 these policies (at any rate in the case of the Soviet Union) were shifting their emphasis from promoting revolution to cultivating friendship. Most of the Soviet aid has been going to India, the United Arab Republic and Iran.[9]

Some of the Communist aid has been provided for projects which the Western powers have refused to undertake. For example, in 1965 the Americans, the British and the World Bank cancelled their commitment to finance the new High Dam at Aswan, in Egypt, so the

Russians provided the money ($325 million), together with other technical and economic aid. "If Egypt ever reaches the 'take-off' point, it will be largely due to the Soviet Union, and there is no reason to doubt President Nasser's sincerity when he declared, at the ceremony to mark the opening of the High Dam diversion canal, that the Egyptian people would never under any circumstances forget the help of Mr. Khrushchev and the Soviet people." [10] Similarly, the Chinese were invited by the Tanzanian and Zambian governments to build a railway from Dar es Salaam to the Zambian copper belt, which the Americans, the British and the World Bank had refused to finance because they considered it an uneconomic proposition.

By the end of the sixties, therefore, something of an impasse had been reached in the field of aid. On the one hand, the gulf between the rich and the poor countries was inexorably widening; trade and investment were failing to narrow it; the need for aid was greater than ever. The tools of aid, the surveys and statistics, were accumulating, and some of the worst mistakes were being rectified by donors and recipients. But on the other hand, there was growing disillusionment, in both rich and poor countries, with the whole operation, for reasons discussed in Chapter 15.

Such was the situation when the Second United Nations Development Decade was launched in 1970.

References

1. Lester B. Pearson (Chairman), *Partners in Development, Report of the Commission on International Development to the World Bank* (London: Pall Mall Press, Ltd., 1969), p. 137.

2. OECD figures.

3. Isaiah Frank, "International Trade Policy for the Second Development Decade," in the *International Journal of the Canadian Institute for International Affairs*, Vol. 25, No. 1, Winter 1969–70, pp. 97–98.

4. Robert S. McNamara, *Address to the United Nations Conference on Trade and Development, Santiago, Chile,* April 14, 1972 (Washington, D.C.: International Bank for Reconstruction and Development), p. 11.

5. Lester B. Pearson, *op. cit.,* p. 77.

6. *The Economist* (London), November 1, 1969.

7. "Nations in Need: A Special Report on Aid to Developing Countries," *The Times* (London), September 14, 1971, p. 11. (OECD and United Nations figures.)

8. Sir Robert Jackson, *A Study of the Capacity of the United Nations' Development System,* Vol. I (Geneva, Switzerland: United Nations, 1969).

9. Robert C. Jaster, "Foreign Aid and Economic Development: The Shifting Soviet View," in *International Affairs,* Vol. 45, No. 3, July 1969 (London: The Royal Institute of International Affairs); OECD figures; and *The Economist* (London), November 6, 1971, p. 66.

10. Peter Mansfield, *Nasser's Egypt* (Middlesex, England: Penguin Books, Ltd., 1965), p. 1.

fifteen

THE SECOND
DEVELOPMENT DECADE

During the First Development Decade the poor countries fulfilled their 5 percent growth target, but the rich countries did not fulfill the 1 percent of GNP target for financing development in the poor countries. Although the flow of governmental aid and private funds nearly doubled, rising from $8.6 billion in 1960–62 to $14.7 billion in 1970, their GNP increased at a faster rate, so that the proportion of GNP transferred fell from 0.95 percent in 1961 to 0.74 percent in 1970. Governmental aid, moreover, declined from 0.52 to 0.34 percent of GNP; and promises to "untie" aid were not kept. Up until 1969 United States aid accounted for half of the total supplied by the 16 member countries of the OECD, although it amounted to a declining proportion of the American GNP. In 1970 the American proportion fell to 40 percent[1] and it has continued to fall.

In the face of this flagging performance, and armed with the long-term assessments and recommendations of the World Bank's Pearson Report, the General Assembly of the United Nations adopted by acclamation, in October 1970, a Development Strategy for the Second United Nations' Decade, which set new targets for growth by the poor countries and for aid from the rich countries.

The poor countries' target is an overall growth rate of 6 percent, and a per capita rate of 3.5 percent—for this time the population explosion is taken into account: a population growth rate of 2.5 percent is assumed. This 3.5 percent growth rate would "represent a doubling of average income per head in the course of two decades." A specific target is that the poor countries will expand expenditure on research and development to 0.5 percent of their GNP by 1980.

The rich countries are again asked to transfer a minimum of 1 percent of their GNP by 1972, or at the latest, by 1975; to increase the component of governmental aid to 0.7 percent of the 1 percent by 1975; to "untie" bilateral aid, to "soften" the terms of loans and to prevent debt crises arising in the poor countries' repayments of loans. The volume of aid given through multilateral channels should be increased "to the fullest extent possible." (This constitutes an evasion of the Pearson Report's recommendation for a specific increase from 10 to 20 percent.) The rich countries "will substantially increase their aid for the direct support of science and technology in the developing countries during the decade," and will, in 1973, consider setting a target percentage of their GNP for this purpose. The poor countries attach great importance to this measure, which would begin to free them from "technological colonialism." [2] At present one percent of all the research and development in the world is devoted to the problems of the poor countries, while 50 percent is devoted to military and space matters.[3] The document outlines, for the first time, a *global development strategy*, in which the rich and the poor countries would cooperate as partners in promoting integrated and comprehensive development. It proposes *qualitative* objectives relating to education, health, nutrition, reform of land tenure, housing and employment, and affirms that growth must be accompanied by social justice, so that its benefits may be shared by all.

Finally, the document was interpreted by the poor countries, and accepted by the majority of the rich countries, as constituting "a moral and political commitment." [4] It was described by the "Group of Seventy-Seven" poor countries as "the best possible reflection of the present stage of the collective conscience of mankind in one of the most crucial areas of organizing human society." [5] The Soviet bloc made dissenting noises about the need to ensure that development takes place in the context of socialist policies.

By the end of 1972 the rich countries had shown no serious intention of implementing their "moral and political commitment." The total level of governmental aid given by the OECD countries rose from 0.34 percent of their GNP in 1970 to 0.35 percent in 1971.[6] Commenting on this performance, Mr. McNamara, President of the World Bank, said: "The collective GNP of the developed countries in 1970 totaled roughly $2,000 billion. In constant prices, it is projected to grow to at least $3,000 billion by 1980." So, "in order to raise the current [OECD] flows of 0.35 percent to the targeted 0.7 percent, the developed countries would need to devote only about 1.5 percent of the amount by which they themselves will grow richer during the decade. The remaining 98.5 percent will provide them with sufficient funds to meet their domestic priorities. . . . Are we to say seriously that these wealthy countries cannot reach the . . . target of 0.7 percent of their combined GNPs? It is manifestly not a case of their not being able to afford it." [7]

It will be recalled that in 1970 world expenditure on armaments reached the level of over $200 billion. A United Nations report of 1971 stated that: "It would take only a 5 percent shift of current expenditure on arms to development to make it possible to approach the official targets for aid. A more substantial curtailment of the arms race would permit for the first time the kind of massive transfer of resources which could make a fundamental change in the prospects for social and economic development. The volume of fixed investment in the developing countries is estimated to have been around $65 billion in 1969. A shift of 10 percent from world military expenditure to investment would provide enough resources to raise the figure by almost one third." [8]

The hardening of the rich countries' attitude towards their "moral commitment" was brought into the open at the third meeting of UNCTAD, which took place at Santiago, Chile, in April–May 1972. At the two previous meetings, held in 1964 and 1968, the rich countries were prepared to make some concessions. At Santiago, however, their attitude was mainly defensive. They rejected or sidetracked demands from the poor countries for more agreements to stabilize the prices of primary products; for further reduction of tariffs and of nontariff trade barriers; for assistance to help them to diversify their exports; for some measure of debt relief; for an international code to regulate shipping charges which would take their interests into account (the poor countries own only 7.4 percent of the world's shipping, but provide 41 percent of the world's bulk cargoes); for the reform of the international monetary system in their interests (see Chapter 16); for the untying of aid; and for a commitment to meet the aid targets of the Second Development Decade. Their excuse for stalling on trade liberalization and monetary reform was that these subjects would be dealt with in GATT and the IMF—bodies in which they have a larger influence. They also rejected an UNCTAD scheme for "market sharing," under which they would allocate a proportion of their markets to the poor countries by cutting back their own protected production. The Director-General of the FAO estimated that if the rich countries reduced their self-sufficiency in temperate agricultural products by 2 percent, this would make available to the poor countries a share in their market amounting to four billion dollars a year. But the rich countries asserted that market sharing would interfere with the working of the free-enterprise system. The only concrete achievement of UNCTAD III was an agreement by the rich countries to increase their aid to twenty-five of the poorest (and smallest) of the poor countries (sixteen in Africa, eight in Asia and the Middle East, and Haiti in the Western hemisphere) by 50 percent, but without commitment *not* to cut aid to the slightly less poor proportionately.[9]

The poor countries, for their part, did not play their hand very well at the Conference. They did not present a united front; and they made too many demands, some of them irrelevant. The Chinese, who were present for the first time, adopted a restrained posture, as if anxious to find their feet in the international arena before asserting themselves as the leaders of the poor countries' trade union.

UNCTAD III thus dealt a severe blow to the idea of a world development strategy in which rich and poor would cooperate as "partners in development."

The Second Development Decade strategy is based on the assumption of the Pearson Report that the policy pursued for the past two decades of bridging the gulf between the rich and the poor countries by limited trade concessions and relatively small amounts of aid will, if somewhat expanded, bring the poor countries within two or three more decades to the take-off point for self-development. As Mr. Mcnamara has pointed out, this policy is not going to hurt the rich countries. Why, then, are they refusing to commit themselves to it?

First, there is a general disillusionment with aid. The substantial achievements—the useful capital projects which have sprouted all over the poor countries; the valuable surveys of most major problems; the vital research which has, for example, produced the Green Revolution—are overshadowed in the public and often in the official mind by the glaring failures: the unrepaired tractors rusting in the fields; the unneeded prestige projects; the waste and incompetence and corruption. Critics in the rich countries overlook the fact that they themselves are partly responsible for these failures by giving their aid in uncoordinated and partisan ways, by not relating it fully to the developing countries' real needs, which in many countries are now more clearly identifiable as planning techniques improve.

There is also a more fundamental reason for disillusionment. It can be argued that a good deal of aid has been counterproductive, or, as the poor countries put it, "imperialistic," in relation to the real goals of development, because it has been supplied to regimes which are more anxious to promote quantitative economic growth through rapid industrialization, which benefits the elite, than to carry out social reforms which benefit the masses. The establishment of a government dedicated to social justice may involve the replacement of a feudal or conservative middle-class regime by a socialistic one, perhaps by force. Socialistic regimes expropriate the private companies of the rich countries. Fear of expropriation and of "communism," which may involve Russian or Chinese economic and political infiltration, impels Western aid-giving governments to bolster up the reactionary regimes, often against their better judgment. The twenty billion dollars in aid offered to Latin American countries by the United States under the Alliance for Progress of 1961 was, for example, made conditional upon the carrying out of land tenure, taxation, health and educational reforms. But regimes such as those of Chile and Peru, which have been seriously undertaking such reforms, have disqualified themselves for American aid by their expropriation policies, while right-wing dictatorships such as those of Brazil, South Korea and the Philippines, which have pushed up economic growth at the expense of social progress, have received substantial aid. Even international capital-aid organizations such as the World Bank and the International Monetary Fund (IMF), whose objectives are strictly non-political, are affected by this attitude, since they raise their funds through and operate within the free-enterprise economy. They are thus naturally inclined to help governments which concentrate on financial stability and economic growth—which may involve neglecting social policies. The World Bank has, however, latterly shown increasing recognition of the need to balance capital development with social projects.

Soviet and East European aid policies are "imperialistic" in a different way. They aim at tying the recipient country's economy to their own by exacting payment in locally produced goods, such as Egyptian and Sudanese cotton, which they buy cheap and then unload on the world markets at higher prices. The recipient country is thus prevented from earning hard currency, and at the same time may be forced to buy Communist goods at inflated prices. "Economic self-interest is the virtually declared objective of Soviet policy." [12]

To some extent, therefore, aid may be exacerbating rather than solving the real problems of the poor countries. The foreign minister of Zaire told the United Nations General Assembly in October 1972 that "the attitudes of the industrialised countries had prompted his own country to decide to resort to foreign assistance 'only when absolutely necessary.' " [13] Meanwhile, many people in the rich countries resent the ingratitude of the poor without understanding its cause.

To the general disillusionment with aid another factor must now be added: the waning of the Cold War is removing the political motive for giving aid. The First and Second Worlds no longer need to woo the Third World. The superpowers—the United States, the Soviet Union, West Europe, Japan and China—are now (in 1973), preoccupied with developing new relationships with each other, based essentially on trade; and the poor countries seem to be dropping out of the picture. It remains to be seen whether China, containing one-third of the population of the developing world, will provide the leadership to bring them back into the limelight.

Finally, the mood of the rich countries at UNCTAD III was conditioned by their preoccupation with their own internal problems of mounting inflation and unemployment (see Chapter 3). There was a feeling that until their own economies were growing healthily again they could not commit themselves to doing much more for the poor countries.

It is possible, however, that the power politics and internal preoccupations of the rich countries may soon be as out of date as the ideologies of the cold war. For casting long shadows over the world scene are two newly recognized problems of global import: the rapid depletion of world resources in relation to world needs, taking the population explosion into account; and the simultaneous pollution of the planet by overconsumption in the rich countries. The solution to both problems may call for some sort of planetary economic management, or "housekeeping," as it is coming to be called, of world resources in the common interest. The very idea of the transfer of some resources from some rich countries to some poor ones may soon be anachronistic. Lester Pearson has called the world a "global village"; and as in traditional villages, all its resources may have to be administered as a trust for all its inhabitants.

References

1. OECD figures.

2. Command Paper 4568: *An International Development Strategy for the Second United Nations' Development Decade, with Related Documents* (London: Her Majesty's Stationery Office, 1971).

3. Information from the Voluntary Committee on Aid and Development, London, 1971.

4. Command Paper 4568, *op. cit.*, p. 6.

5. *Ibid.*, p. 29.

6. OECD figures.

7. Robert S. McNamara, *Address to the United Nations Conference on Aid and Development*, Santiago, Chile, April 14, 1972 (Washington, D.C.: World Bank pamphlet), p. 9.

8. United Nations, *Economic and Social Consequences of the Arms Race and of Military Expenditures*, Report of the Secretary-General, 1972 (A/8469, Rev. 1).

9. World Development Movement, *End of an Illusion: Verdict on UNCTAD III* (London: Voluntary Committee on Aid and Development pamphlet, July 1972).

10. See Teresa Hayter, *Aid as Imperialism* (Middlesex, England: Penguin Books, Ltd., 1971).

11. Speech by Mr. McNamara to the Economic and Social Council of the United Nations, October 18, 1972.

12. *The Economist* (London), November 6, 1971, pp. 66–67.

13. *The New York Times,* October 4, 1972.

sixteen

TOWARD A WORLD
MONETARY SYSTEM

The world's monetary system is organized on an essentially national basis. Each government issues its own currency, providing paper notes and metal coins, as it sees fit, and exercises some degree of control over the total means of payment, including bank credits. The relationship of national currencies to gold was loosened after World War I, although the United States continued until 1971 to express the value of the dollar in terms of gold, and to be prepared to transfer gold to foreign central banks against dollars. Modern policies of "managing" the economy, discussed in Chapter 3, aim at ensuring that the amount of currency produced by national banks is related to money incomes. In free-enterprise countries expansion of demand is facilitated by credit: national and private banks hold reserves of currency for this purpose. When governments think it desirable to accelerate economic expansion—in order, for example, to promote employment—they reduce taxation, expand credit facilities and sometimes embark on public works and other forms of government expenditure. But when the expansion of money exceeds the production of goods and services—for example, as a result of wage increases—inflation may occur, and governments may have to take measures to dampen down demand by higher taxation, the restriction of credit, the curbing of wages and prices, the scaling down of government expenditure and so on.

International trade obviously has to be underpinned by arrangements for the convertibility of one national currency into another, and by the creation of international credit resources—the "liquidity problem." The failure to deal with this problem was a factor in causing the Great Depression of 1929–33, in which world trade shrank by a quarter, and in encouraging the ensuing policies of financial "autarchy," in which governments resorted, to a considerable extent, to barter arrangements.

In 1945 the International Monetary Fund (IMF) was set up to provide on an international basis a limited measure of the monetary control and support which governments provide for their citizens on a national basis—to be a kind of "Central Bank for central banks." [1] All member states (some one hundred twenty-five in 1973) contribute a quota related to their GNP, their foreign trade and their monetary reserves. Since 1945 the Fund has loaned to member states the equivalent of over twenty billion dollars to help them in their monetary troubles.[1]

The great expansion of international trade which has taken place since 1945 has been the result of the removal of tariffs and other trade barriers. It has been made possible by a general restoration of the convertibility of one currency into another and of a measure of international liquidity. Both factors were, until 1971, based on the "gold exchange standard." Under the Bretton Woods Agreement of 1944, which set up the IMF, national currencies were related to the dollar, which alone was directly related to gold at the fixed rate of thirty-five dollars to the ounce. Reserves of gold, dollars and sterling held in the central banks of the rich countries made it possible to provide for a great expansion of the volume of credit and currency for international trade.

There were obvious weaknesses in this system. First, the economic fate of all countries involved (that is, more or less all the countries of the world except the Communist countries, which have closed monetary systems, and which, except for Yugoslavia, are not members of the IMF) depended on the way the dollar, and to a lesser extent the pound, were managed by the American and British governments. If they accumulated large reserves and did not correspondingly extend their purchases from the rest of the world, they might retard development in other countries. If, on the other hand, they imported too much or invested too much abroad, confidence in their ability to meet claims which might be made on them would be shaken. In either case, other countries had no control over policies which vitally affected them, and which might be dictated by considerations of national interest or international politics. In the late sixties, France made a major protest at the excessive influence of the United States on the world's monetary system.

Second, although the IMF has machinery for altering exchange rates "in cases of fundamental disequilibrium," it has not been able to prevent its members' inflation and/or balance of payments problems from causing recurrent international financial crises, in which some of the rich countries have been forced to take snap decisions to devalue or to revalue. These crises, which have intensified since 1967, have, however, been prevented from escalating into a major world depression like that of 1929–33 by ad hoc international action taken through the Group of Ten—an informal body representing the leading industrial nations of the Western world, the IMF, and the OECD.

Third, the amount of international liquidity—the reserve funds of dollars and sterling—in the banks of the rich countries is inadequate to provide a credit basis for expanding international trade. The policy of keeping reserves stable by pegging them to the dollar and the dollar to gold means that "one country can increase its reserves only at the expense of another." [2]

Before 1914 Britain was perhaps the only major country which depended for its survival on international trade. By the early seventies, global commercial interdependence had reached a point when the outlines of a global economy were emerging. The fact that all monetary transactions through which the global trading system operates are still based on national monetary systems controlled by national governments is inevitably causing increasing difficulties. By 1971 convertibility problems were fomenting "creeping protectionism"; and the necessity for the United States to reduce its trade imbalance produced a crisis which led to the President's decision to ask Congress to devalue the dollar in relation to gold for the first time in thirty years, and to the temporary suspension of its gold convertibility. In February 1973 a further devaluation took place. The linchpin which held the whole system together was beginning to snap. The need for a reform of the international monetary system was becoming apparent. In December 1971 the Group of Ten and the IMF agreed that "they would have to consider reform of the international monetary system over the longer term." [3]

A first step in this direction was taken in 1969, when the IMF established a system of 9.5 billion units of "Special Drawing Rights." These are financial assets, defined in terms of gold but independent of gold and of national currencies, which are created by the IMF— the first time that an international body has created money—and allocated to the participating member countries in relation to their quotas. A member can convert its SDRs into the currencies of other participants designated by the IMF. The SDRs are not exactly money, because they can be used only between governments; and they are not exactly credit. They are "intended to provide a means whereby the growth of world reserves can be adjusted to the expression of production and trade in an orderly and deliberate fashion" [4] by creating a system whereby a country can create reserves without a surrender of real resources. It has been suggested that "ten or twelve years from now [1970] the amount of SDRs in the world's bank reserves will be almost equal to the amount of gold so held. . . . One could hazard a guess . . . that the world's monetary reserves might consist of one third gold, one third SDRs and one third foreign currencies and reserve positions in the IMF. In this way the world's needs for basic banking reserves could be adequately taken care of for years to come." [5] There would, however, remain the problem of the "adjustment" of currencies to each other.

Hitherto the poor countries have been, in the words of M. Pierre-Paul Schweitzer, the former Managing Director of the IMF, "helpless bystanders and victims" of the unstable international monetary structure. The dollar devaluation of 1971, for example, decreased the purchasing power of their dollar assets in terms of other currencies. But they are not members of the Group of Ten; they were not consulted when the financial crisis occurred; and their interests were not considered in the measures taken to deal with it. Because their quotas in the IMF are small, their share in the SDRs is only about 28 percent. They have been demanding that the IMF should replace the Group of Ten as the central forum in which world monetary policy is handled; that they should receive a greater share of the SDRs; and that a link should be established between the SDRs and development aid, so that the former could be partially used to finance the latter. Their proposal is that their SDRs should be increased above the level of their quotas, in order to provide them with additional credit in the rich countries, or additional development finance through the International Development Association of the World Bank. In May 1972 the rich countries agreed to supplement the Group of Ten by a Group of Twenty, which includes nine poor countries, whose particular task is to study proposals for international monetary reform. And at UNCTAD III the rich countries agreed to study the proposals for linking the SDRs to development aid.

The nations of the world are therefore now aware that the national monetary systems through which their economies operate must be welded into an international structure, providing for credit and convertibility; and since this is in the particular interests of the poor countries as a means of promoting their development, they are likely to exert increasing pressure on the rich countries to move forward.

References

1. W. Randolph Burgess and James Robert Huntley, *Europe and America, The Next Ten Years* (New York: Walker & Company, 1970), p. 94.

2. United Nations Conference on Trade and Development, *International Monetary Reform and Cooperation for Development* (New York: United Nations, 1969), p. 6.

3. Press Communiqué of the Ministerial Meeting of the Group of Ten, Washington, D.C., December 18, 1971.

4. United Nations Conference on Trade and Development, *op. cit.*, p. 13.

5. W. Randolph and James Robert Huntley, *ibid.*, p. 100.

seventeen

THE PROBLEM OF
FOOD RESOURCES

We have already seen in Chapter 8 that FAO estimates that 3–500 million people in the poor countries do not eat enough food, and that 1.5 billion (excluding China) do not receive an adequately balanced diet. On the other hand, an increasing number of people in the rich countries (especially in those of Western Europe and North America) have a diet too rich and substantial for good health. The rich countries' good diet is based on three factors. First, as a whole, they produce more food of most kinds than they need even to meet their present high standards of consumption (Britain and the Soviet Union are exceptions); second, they can afford to import food, either from each other or from the poor countries; and third, their populations are growing at a third the rate of those of the poor countries.

The basic aims of the poor countries for food production are three-fold: first, to raise nutritional standards for their exploding populations—they will have a billion more mouths to feed by 1985; second, to achieve self-sufficiency—whereas before World War II they were net exporters of cereals, now they are net importers, the quantities imported having trebled between 1949 and 1968 (30–40 percent of these imports were "food aid" from the rich countries, especially the United States); and third, to increase their exports to the rich countries of both raw and processed foodstuffs—especially of noncereal crops such as sugar, bananas, cocoa, coffee and oilseeds—in order to earn the foreign exchange with which to buy industrial equipment. What are the possibilities that they can achieve these aims?

At the instigation of the First World Food Conference, convened by FAO in 1963, the FAO produced, in 1969, *The Provisional Indicative World Plan for Agricultural Development*. This document, (which we will call the FAO Plan) assesses the food needs of the poor countries and the possibilities of meeting these needs by 1985. (It does not deal with the rich countries nor with Communist China.)

The planners estimate that, in general, the demand for food in the poor countries will have increased two and a half times between 1962 and 1985. Over two-thirds of this increase will be the result of population growth, and less than one-third the result of the growth of family incomes, that is, of increased prosperity.

The planners think that it may be possible for the poor countries to achieve a breakthrough in cereal production by 1985; if their targets are met, calorie supplies in the poor countries would be adequate, although many people would still be undernourished unless present inequalities in the distribution of income can be reduced. They see no realistic possibility of closing the protein gap with animal protein. A further development of the "Green Revolution" (see below) may help to close it with vegetable protein.

Most authorities are agreed that, except in tropical areas, the limits of the *amount* of land which can be brought under cultivation on the planet are in sight. As regards the rich countries, there is considerable scope for expansion in North America—in 1969 only 50 percent of the potential arable acreage of the continent was being cultivated [1]—but until 1972 cultivation was deliberately held back because existing production outstripped demand (see below). In the poor countries, on the other hand, the area under cultivation was expanded by 21 percent between 1948 and 1959, and by 11 percent between 1959 and 1966.[2] It is significant that four-fifths of the increase in production came from taking this new land under cultivation. The Plan assumes an expansion of cultivated land from 1,407 million acres in 1962 to 1,653 million acres in 1985, by which time the countries of Southeast Asia and North Africa will, it is estimated, have brought all their potential cultivatable land into use, and the countries of the rest of Asia and of Latin America 80 percent of theirs. There remain the deserts in the Sahara and elsewhere, and the tropical areas which constitute 40 percent of the surface of Africa and Latin America. It may be possible to cultivate some of the deserts, either by tapping underground waters, as is being done on a large scale in the Punjab areas of India and Pakistan (a great underground lake is thought to exist under the Sahara), or eventually by piping desalinated sea water to them. The exploitation of tropical lands, where there is water as well as sunshine, is a more immediate practical possibility. Basic research must, however, first be carried out—hitherto tropical agricultural research has concentrated on industrial crops. When projects for clearing and cultivating the tropical soil were started in East Africa and Brazil, the soil turned to a rocklike consistency. It has been suggested that these soils would be best utilized by retaining the ground cover and cultivating vegetables underneath it, but the indigenous crops such as yams, bananas, sago and tapioca lack protein; the seed-bearing cereals which have good protein content need dry weather in which to ripen.[3]

It can be argued that in some countries more land has already been brought under cultivation than is healthy from the point of view of maintaining the ecology of the biosphere. Certain countries, notably China and India, and the Andean states of Latin America, have through the centuries largely destroyed their forests, thus producing serious soil erosion, with its attendant floods and droughts. The United States and the Soviet Union, in the twenties and the fifties respectively, created vast dust bowls by rashly ploughing up large areas of grassland. They remedied the situation by leaving millions of acres fallow, so that the soil could accumulate moisture again, and by planting thousands of miles of windbreaks. The poor countries cannot afford to take large areas out of cultivation, and they do not have the technical skills nor the financial resources for the immense projects involved—although China has made a start.

When the possibilities of bringing new land under cultivation are exhausted, there are two other ways of increasing the production of plant foodstuffs. The first is to increase the yields of the crops grown on the existing cultivated land, and the second is to cultivate pasture land at the expense of animal raising.

Science is being applied to improving the yields from cultivated land in five main ways: by plant breeding, the application of chemical fertilizers, the use of pesticides to control weeds and insects, irrigation and mechanization. While the area cultivated in the rich countries has remained relatively static, their crop yields per hectare increased by 19 percent between 1948 and 1959 and 18 percent between 1959 and 1966. Japan's crop yields are four to five times those of India.[4] In the poor countries there is immense scope for increasing yields, which, according to the Director-General of the FAO, must be regarded as "imperative for survival."

A major breakthrough in the breeding of wheat, maize and rice occurred in the late fifties and early sixties. Plant breeders working in the Rockefeller and Ford Foundation research stations in Mexico and the Philippines crossed local strains with strains imported from the United States, Japan, Taiwan and elsewhere, and from this mixture of the indigenous and the alien produced new strains which are short-statured, stiff-stemmed, early maturing and highly responsive to chemical fertilizers. In 1968 these strains were grown on 5 percent of the earth's cereal area, and the first results were dramatic. Not only were some yields doubled, notably in Mexico and in the Punjab states of

India and Pakistan, but it was possible, where water supplies were adequate, to harvest two, three of four crops a year. "India's production of wheat expanded 50 percent between 1965 and 1969. In the spring of 1968, village schools were closed in much of northern India, simply because the buildings were needed to store a record crop of wheat." [5] By 1971 the area planted to the new varieties covered some 10 percent of the estimated cultivated area of Asia (excluding China, which has been researching independently in this field): this involved some 20 percent of the wheat acreage and 10 percent of that of rice. In 1971 the wheat crops of India and Pakistan were double those of 1965—a favorable year. The "new technology" has not yet had a substantial impact in Latin America, except in Mexico, where the average Mexican now consumes 40 percent more food than before it was introduced, nor in Africa, except in limited areas in the north and east.[6] And in 1972 there were serious setbacks in production in a number of Asian countries, due to too much rain in some, and too little in others.[7] The monsoon rains were inadequate in India, so that by early 1973 the large stocks accumulated in the previous bumper years were being used up, and imports of two million tons of wheat were being arranged.[8] The significance of this setback for future production prospects is not yet clear.

Thus was inaugurated the "Green Revolution." A ray of bright light has shot across the dark horizon of the poor countries' food situation. The chief scientist of the team, the American Dr. Norman E. Borlaug, was awarded the Nobel Peace Prize of 1970 for his work. He announced that he was now working to develop a new tough strain of maize which would contain one of the basic components of protein, the amino acid lycine, which is lacking in ordinary cereals. FAO estimates that the new strains might be grown in a third of the cereal area of the poor countries by 1985. The Green Revolution could help to close the protein gap, partly because it would increase the supplies of vegetable protein, and partly because surpluses of cereals could be used for feeding livestock.

The new seeds, planted in existing conditions, will produce higher yields than the old. But they will only *revolutionize* yields if they are well fertilized, protected by pesticides and, above all, well watered— and this, in many countries, such as India, involves the massive development of irrigation and of energy.[9] "At present, power available per hectare from all sources—human, animal and mechanical—in these countries is far less than the minimum required for achieving optimum yields," says the FAO Report for 1971. Ten times more energy is needed in Africa, three times more in Asia and twice the present quantity in Latin America.[10] The new strains are also introducing more complex problems. In Tunisia, the planting of the short-stemmed Mexican wheat resulted in a serious loss of straw for animal feed, and a lack of humus, producing dry and friable soil and a break in the natural biological cycle, which had to be remedied by the application of large quantities of fertilizers.[11] There are also the dangers that resistance to diseases which are being bred into the plants may collapse, causing massive crop failures, and that meanwhile the germ plasm of the old varieties, the raw material of the breeders, may be irretrievably lost. FAO experts have warned that international action to conserve the germ plasm of many of the world's crops through organized seed collection and storage is urgent; on it may depend the existence of man's future food supplies.[12] The United Nations Conference on the Environment, held in Stockholm in 1972, set in train action on this matter (see Chapter 21). Finally, institutional changes are necessary. In the Far East the preponderance of small farms and the lack of agricultural services is an impediment to the new technology.[13]

Perhaps the greatest achievement of the Green Revolution lies in its psychological impact. According to Dr. Borlaug, "It has installed the spirit of hope where there was complete despair before. Wherever you go you can see people sort of catch fire and begin to believe in themselves. The problem is to keep it going. It's just a spark at present. And it can buy only a very little time in which to adjust population growth to reasonable levels." [14]

Chemical fertilizers, which consist basically of nitrogen, potassium and phosphates, came into widespread use in Europe early in the twentieth century, and in North America after about 1940. As a result yields doubled, trebled and quadrupled. By 1970 their use accounted for a quarter of the world's food supply; the rich third of the world's population, consuming three-quarters of the world's fertilizer production, depended on them for survival.[15]

There is no shortage of nitrates, which by the Haber process are "fixed" artificially from the nitrogen in the air. The earth has plentiful supplies of the mineral potassium; but reserves of phosphates are limited. The recycling of sewage, in which phosphates at present drain off into the sea, is therefore important to agricultural production. The FAO plan advocates a rapid expansion of the use of fertilizers in the poor countries, from a total of 2.6 million tons in 1962 to 28.6 million tons in 1985; even so, they would still be using less fertilizers than the rich countries used in 1965. At present India and China, in particular, are straining every nerve to establish fertilizer plants. India increased its production from nil in 1947 to 750,000 tons in 1969, and was planning to use 5½ million tons by 1974, of which 80 percent would be domestically produced.[16] In 1970 the poor countries as a whole were importing 50 percent of their fertilizer needs.[17] Fertilizer production requires a great deal of water and energy. It takes the amount of energy derived from burning 5 tons of coal to produce one ton of nitrogen fertilizer.[18] Dr. Borlaug told his audience, when he accepted the Nobel Peace Prize, that his dream is to breed cereals which will, like legumes, fix nitrogen from the air and thus eliminate the need for nitrogen fertilizers.

Global preharvest losses from weeds, insects, plant and animal diseases and pests are estimated to have amounted in 1965 to over 35 percent of all agricultural produce, and to fifty billion dollars in value, equal to that of the entire proposed increase in crop output to meet the 1985 targets. The United States spends ten billion dollars a year on pest control. The Plan provides for an increase in expenditure on pesticides in the poor countries from one hundred eighty million dollars in 1965 to two billion dollars in 1985. As regards the ecological dangers of pesticides, FAO has pointed out that the amounts needed by the poor countries by 1985 under the Plan would still be less than the amounts used in the rich countries in 1970. The planners state that "the banning of DDT in developing countries [would] only set back their development efforts without touching the real core of the overall pollution problem."

In the nineteenth century the irrigated area of the world expanded over fivefold, from 20 to 112.5 million acres. By 1965 it had leapt forward to 450 million acres, of which 180 million were in the poor countries, other than China, and no less than 185 million in China.[19] FAO planners assume that the poor countries (other than China) will increase their irrigated area to 273 million acres by 1985. Expenditure on irrigation, the major key to the Green Revolution, accounts for three-quarters of the $48 billion, which is the Plan's estimate of the cost of its proposals for land and water development. (By contrast, the irrigated area of the rich countries is only 89 million acres; "Enough water now falls on North America to supply all its needs.")[20]

About half the irrigation in the poor countries is based on small-scale works—field ditches to distribute the water of ponds and rivulets and to spread the water drawn up from innumerable wells. The expansion of output from these wells has been increased by the substitution of electric or diesel pumps for the slow toil of oxen, which in turn has released for cultivation the pasture on which the oxen fed. As long as underground water resources last—and they are largely unmapped—this kind of irrigation is likely to be a very promising development. The other half of the irrigated land derives from giant dams built to control whole river systems, often involving the creation of artificial lakes. Their aim is not only to increase the amount of water available for the land, but, by controlling the flow, to prevent the floods and droughts which have wrought so much havoc in the past; and also to provide water power for electricity, and thus promote the industrialization of whole regions. Examples are the new high dam at Aswan in Upper Egypt, built by the Russians, which it is hoped will transform Egypt's agriculture and economy, increasing its national income by 40 percent a year;[21] and the Volta River project, in Ghana, built by a consortium of Western companies, which is planned to provide sufficient power for Ghana's neighbours as well as itself, and thus promote the regional unification of Africa. A sad result of politics is the need to spend enormous sums on huge irrigation works in Pakistan and the Indian State of Punjab, because the frontier between the two countries, created in 1947, has split in two the old irrigation system based on the Indus and its five tributaries. The money, which is being provided partly by the World Bank, could be well used to control the waters of the Ganges and the Brahmaputra, and thus provide extra food and safety from droughts and floods for the one hundred forty million people who live in Bangladesh and the Indian State of West Bengal—among the poorest and most densely populated areas in the world.

These great projects have revealed grave ecological problems: the evaporation of water from and the silting up of the reservoirs—the life of some is only twenty to thirty years; the salinization of the soil; and the tendency to provide breeding grounds for the malaria mosquito and the snails which house the parasitic worms which cause bilharzia (schistosomiasis), a disease which debilitates mind and body, and on which little research has been done (see Chapter 8).

Agricultural mechanization must be introduced with discrimination in the poor countries, since a major problem is to find jobs. It is often more appropriate to replace a hoe by an ox-drawn plough than by a tractor, for which fuel and services may not be available. Although 90 percent of the world's tractors are in the rich countries, the total number used in the poor countries nearly doubled in the sixties.

During the sixties the increase in livestock production in the poor countries was less than the increase in population, and in every area except Latin America it fell below the rate achieved in the fifties. Something of an agricultural revolution is needed in this field. First, animal care must be turned into a modern industry. The peasant's herd of two or three cows, which graze on the village pasture by day and shelter in his hut by night, must become a sideline, and what FAO calls "the technique of large-scale production," [22] and the Americans "agribusiness," must be developed. One result of such farming, however, is to reduce the spread of manure in the fields and thus increase the need for fertilizers. Second, the cultivation of feeding stuffs must be expanded. FAO believe that the productivity of grasslands in tropical and temperate areas could be raised five times above the present level, although not by 1985. A breakthrough in meat production therefore depends heavily on a breakthrough in cereal production. Third, animal diseases, which take a toll of some ten million tons of protein a year, must be brought under control.

The Plan recommends that up to 1985 the poor countries should concentrate on increasing poultry and pork supplies, which at present constitute a quarter of their meat production. This, together with the expansion of beef and veal production, could close the gap between the supply and demand for meat. But to achieve this, feed-grain consumption in the poor countries would have to be increased from twenty million tons in 1962 to eighty to ninety million tons in 1985.

The main shortage which the planners see little possibility of meeting is that of the poor countries' milk needs, estimated at thirty-four million tons. If millions of babies are not to be undernourished, this deficit will have to be met by the rich countries, which have ample surplus capacity.

Research into the food resources of the oceans, which cover three-quarters of the earth's surface, suggests a potential harvest of one hundred fifty to two hundred million tons a year in the deep waters—sufficient to meet the protein requirements of both rich and poor countries at 1985 population levels.[23] These waters are at present a free-for-all (see Chapter 20), and the rich countries, led by Japan and the Soviet Union, are deploying large-scale mechanized methods, such as floating fish factories, to get all the fish that they can out of them for their own markets. The world fish catch reached a record level of sixty-two million tons in 1970.[24] Although Peru is the leading fishing nation, most of its catch is sold to the rich countries, much of it to be used as fish meal for animal feed, to augment the already overrich protein diet of many of their inhabitants and their pets. The Peruvians cannot afford at present to eat the fish they catch themselves, because they must earn foreign exchange to buy vitally needed equipment in the rich countries. "But sooner or later," says Dr. Borgstrom, one of America's leading food experts, "the hungry world will want to keep its own protein." The planners estimate that by 1985 the poor countries' demand for fish will amount to about one hundred million tons, of which over a third will be for animal food. Of this, twenty million tons could come from fresh waters, some of it bred in the huge artificial lakes created by the new dams. On a global basis, therefore, the demand *could* be met. But at present the rich countries are diminishing stocks by overfishing and by killing the fish through polluting the waters. And FAO fears that the poor countries will not be able to afford the sophisticated equipment, nor be able to import fish from the rich countries, and that long before stocks are exhausted, marginal costs of production will have risen to a point where it will no longer be profitable to expand fishing.[25] Meanwhile, they urge that the ocean fisheries should be "managed" in the common interest—aquaculture should complement agriculture—so that the poor countries can be assured of this vital source of protein. "Oceanic fisheries are, by and large, a common property resource," say the planners, "and an increasing number of stocks are, in the absence of prompt and effective action, likely to be over-exploited by 1985." [26] A British Government Report prepared for the United Nations Conference on the Environment (see Chapter 21) makes the same point. Although there is an elaborate structure of international and domestic regulations on such matters as minimum mesh and landing sizes, "limitation of fishing effort remains the central problem." Fishing will not provide large quantities of cheap protein until there is "controlled harvesting of an unpolluted sea." [27]

During the past decade there has been much research into new ways of increasing supplies of protein from plants. They range from breeding cereals with a higher protein content to breeding protein-producing bacteria and yeast on the waste products of sugar cane, petroleum, coal and natural gas, and breeding algae in sewage plants and then using the algae, either as an animal feed or as a substratum for the cultivation of yeast and nutritious fungi.[28] The possibility is even being investigated of manufacturing proteins artificially through "subcellular engineering," based on manipulating the DNA molecule in the chromosomes.[29]

If these experiments with the development of plant protein are successful, the way forward may lie in global vegetarianism, since it takes four to twelve pounds of feed grain to produce a pound of grain-fed meat. A leading nutritionist writes: "There is good reason to think that plant products will supplant animal products as sources of protein when it is realised that they can be produced more economically and are nutritionally adequate. This is an aspect of research that now needs support more than any other." [30] The Director-General of FAO considers that these are "exciting long-range possibilities." They are not expected to have any significant impact within the short-term period of the FAO Plan.

The Plan is realistic, in that it is based on a sober projection of population growth, and on the assumption that the poor countries must basically help themselves, with marginal aid from the rich. It therefore makes the determining factor in its assessment of needs, not "rumbling bellies or crippling protein malnutrition," not some statistical calculation of needs in terms of absolute nutritional standards, but hard cash—the capacity of the citizens of the poor countries to pay for their food.[31] The resulting targets are modest. If they are met, the majority of the 2.5 billion people whom the Plan covers *may* be secured from starvation, and will have a *little* more to eat than the majority in the poor countries eat at present. But the gulf between the well fed and the ill fed in the world will not be bridged. The estimated capital cost is also modest: $112.5 billion over the period 1962–85—$9 billion a year, or 4.5 percent of the current annual world expenditure on armaments. The planners estimate that 40 percent of the capital items involved will have to be imported, involving perhaps an annual cost of $7 billion by 1985—a rather higher figure than that of the total of present governmental aid (see Chapter 15). These imports will have to be paid for, in the main, by exports to the rich countries of tropical agricultural products. As we saw in Chapter 13, the prospects that the rich countries will help the poor countries to expand their markets for these products are not at present bright.

The Director-General of FAO wrote in 1970 that the Plan was intended "to provide a framework within which national and regional programs can develop. . . . It is hoped that it might also form a useful standard of reference for the resolution of conflicts of production and trade policies between nations," and "serve as a guide to both donors and recipients of international aid." But the Plan has not been officially accepted as a target by the international community. The very fact that its title has now been changed to a "Study" indicates that it is regarded as in no way authoritative.

FAO's report on *The State of Food and Agriculture in 1971* makes it clear that the goals of the "Study" are not being fulfilled. In the Middle East and Africa there was no overall increase in food production, so that per capita food consumption *declined*. In Latin America food production just kept even with population growth; only in Asia was food production "comfortably" ahead of population—because of the success of the Green Revolution—but this success is far from secure, as the setback of 1972 has indicated. The overall food situation of the poor countries can only be regarded as menacing. Confronted with this situation, the nations of the world have shelved the only attempt to produce an overall agricultural strategy. Agricultural development in the poor countries continues to take place within the framework of some ninety national plans, loosely coordinated in various regional organizations. And in most of the countries of the world, rich and poor, agricultural production and consumption continue to depend on the market economy, inevitably governed by considerations of short-term profit or loss. Thus, while the poor countries have been struggling desperately to increase their production, the rich countries, whose soaring yields have produced large unsold surpluses, have been reducing theirs: in 1968–69 the United States reduced its acreage under cultivation by a quarter—over fifty million acres, a little more than the total acreage in the poor countries planted with the new seeds; and in 1970 Canada halved its crop acreage.[32] (In 1972 both countries were putting some land back into cultivation, partly as a result of huge Soviet cereal purchases.) The countries of Western Europe have been similarly reducing their production of dairy products. The United States Government has been sending over one billion dollars' worth of surplus food a year to the poor countries as aid; and other aid programs have included agricultural equipment—some of it unsuitable, such as the snow ploughs supplied by the Russians to Guinea; help in building the great irrigation works to which we have referred; and provision of research. But this help, important though it is, cannot bridge the growing gulf between the surplus-ridden and the hunger-ridden nations. The rich countries *could* provide enough food to make up the production deficiencies in the poor countries during the next decade or two, to hold the line until technology has developed new breakthroughs: new kinds of protein, tropical food crops, desalinated water for irrigation and cheap and plentiful energy (see Chapter 19) which could transform their long-term prospects. Will they do so? FAO says, in its 1971 *Report*: "If adjustments are not made in production and trade patterns which reflect superseded comparative advantage and outmoded national aspirations, the entire process of economic and social development, in rich and poor countries alike, will suffer. The completely unbalanced state of world agriculture . . . would, if allowed to persist, slow down world development and might even provoke intensified trade war and destroy patterns of co-operation built up so painfully since 1945. . . . In the world today agricultural policies can no longer be formulated in an exclusively national or even regional or subregional context." "International adjustment" is to be the theme of FAO's 1973 Conference. Another way of putting it would be "international planning."

References

1. United States National Academy of Science—National Research Council, *Resources and Man* (San Francisco, California: W. H. Freeman & Company, 1969), p. 68.

2. *FAO Indicative World Food Plan* (Rome, 1969).

3. N. W. Pirie, *Food Resources Conventional and Novel* (Middlesex, England: Penguin Books, Ltd., 1969), p. 36.

4. Discussion between Dr. Norman Borlaug and Professor Georg Borgstrom, of Michigan University, in *The Observer Review* (London), March 5, 1972.

5. Information Leaflet of the Education Unit, Voluntary Committee on Overseas Aid and Development, London, March 1972.

6. Addeke H. Boerma (Director-General of FAO), "A World Agricultural Plan," in *Scientific American*, August 1970, p. 58; Montague Yudelman, "The Green Revolution," in *OECD Observer*, No. 52, June 1971, p. 16; and *The Observer Review, op. cit.*

7. *The New York Times*, December 12, 1972.

8. *The Manchester Guardian Weekly*, Manchester, England, January 6, 1973.

9. *The Observer Review, op. cit.*

10. FAO, *The State of Food and Agriculture* (Rome, 1971), p. 34.

11. Information given to the author by Sir Edward Warner, former British Ambassador in Tunisia.

12. Sir Otto Frankl, *et al.*, "The Genetic Dangers of the Green Revolution," in *Ceres, FAO Review*, Vol. 2, No. 5, October 1969, pp. 35–37.

13. FAO, *op. cit.*, p. 88.

14. *The Observer Review, op. cit.*

15. Georg Borgstrom, *Too Many: A Study of Earth's Biological Limitations* (London: Mcmillan and Co., 1969), p. 31.

16. Planning Commission, Government of India, *Fourth Five-Year Plan 1969–74*, p. 300.

17. FAO, *op. cit.*, p. 32.

18. *The Observer Review, op. cit.*

19. Georg Borgstrom, *op. cit.*, pp. 185–86.

20. *Ibid.*, p. 186.

21. Information from Sir Geoffrey Furlonge, formerly of the British Foreign Service.

22. FAO, *The State of Food and Agriculture, 1970*, pp. 171–72.

23. Information received from Sir George Deacon, Director of the National Institute of Oceanography, Surrey, England.

24. FAO, *The State of Food and Agriculture*, 1971, p. 15.

25. Addeke H. Boerma, *op. cit.*, p. 58.

26. FAO, *Indicative World Food Plan*, p. 40.

27. *Sinews for Survival: A Report on the Management of Natural Resources to the Secretary of State for the Environment*, February 1972 (London: Her Majesty's Stationery Office, 1972), pp. 23–26.

28. N. W. Pirie, *op. cit.*, Chapters 5, 6 and 7.

29. J. Gordon Theodore, *The Future* (New York: St. Martin's Press, 1965), pp. 32–33.

30. N. W. Pirie, *op. cit.*, p. 114.

31. *The Observer Foreign News Service* (London), No. 27832, June 18, 1970.

32. FAO, *The State of Food and Agriculture, 1971*, p. xi.

eighteen

THE PROBLEM OF MINERAL
AND ENERGY RESOURCES

Minerals extracted from the earth have hitherto supplied most of the raw materials out of which modern industry has fashioned its great works, and fossil fuels the energy which has driven the machines. In providing food, Nature continuously renews herself; but the mineral and fossil fuel resources of the planet are irreplaceable. They are widely and unevenly spread throughout the globe. Before the modern age had dawned two hundred years ago they had barely been tapped. In the past fifty years, however, the world has consumed more of its mineral resources than in the whole of its previous history.[1]

Minerals are, of course, the main substances used by modern industry. They have been extracted haphazardly and indiscriminately from the ground, with individuals, companies and governments grabbing what they can to feed the insistent urge for economic growth. The major consumers are, naturally, the industrialized countries. By the early seventies the annual world consumption of iron ore was 4 times the level of 1950, 85 percent of it occurring in the rich countries.[2] In the late sixties, per capita annual consumption of steel ranged from 700 to 300 kilograms in the rich countries, and from 15 to 10 kilograms or even less in the poor countries. (The figure for the United States in 1967 was 634 kilograms, for India 13.)[3] The United States, with 6 percent of the world's population, accounts for 29 percent of world consumption of 16 main minerals.[4]

Consumption of minerals in rich and poor countries alike is accelerating rapidly—by 50 percent or more a decade. Japan's steel consumption almost quadrupled between 1957 and 1967, and that of the Soviet Union nearly doubled, although the United States' consumption levelled off. At such a rate, starting at this very low base, it will obviously take the poor countries several decades to reach a level of production which would support an adequate standard of living.[5]

Only in the late sixties has a general awareness dawned, not only that mineral resources are irreplaceable, but that they are being rapidly used up. Some of the rich countries have already exhausted their own readily exploitable resources of certain key minerals to the point where they are now dependent on imports. According to a report of the United States National Academy of Sciences, published in 1972, "the United States is almost completely dependent on foreign sources for 22 of the 74 non-energy mineral commodities considered essential for a modern industrial society." [6] The industries of Britain and Japan are almost totally dependent on imported minerals.

How long will the minerals last? In the early seventies a number of estimates are appearing which suggest that if current rates of usage continue to rise exponentially, known reserves of a number of key minerals—copper, mercury, lead, platinum, tin, zinc, gold and silver—may be exhausted by the end of the century or even sooner. Iron and iron-alloy metals—manganese, chromium, nickel, molybdenum, tungsten and cobalt—are expected to last some decades longer.[7] So many uncertain factors are involved, however, that such estimates are best regarded as warning signs of the magnitude and gravity of the problem. New deposits may be discovered, especially in the poor countries, where in a number of cases detailed geological surveys have not yet been carried out. The mineral resources of the oceans may be tapped (see Chapter 20). Rising prices of high-grade ores may stimulate investment in lower grades. The recycling of minerals, which has now started, could be greatly developed. (Britain recycles 40 per cent of the nonferous metals and 56 percent of the lead consumed,[8] and the United States recycles 40 percent of its copper production.)[9] The use of substitutes, such as aluminum (the most abundant mineral in the world) and silicon (sand) could be further expanded. More fundamentally, modern science has discovered the means of reorganizing the very structure of matter, so that completely new materials such as plastics, unknown to nature, are being made.[10] But these possibilities, important and hopeful though they be, are still as uncertain as the estimates of depletion. What is certain is that the world faces a crisis of mineral supplies. The British Ministry of the Environment and the United States National Academy of Sciences are among those who are urging that this crisis calls for international action to explore, conserve and manage the world's mineral resources in the common interest. The National Academy advocates, specifically, planned research by the rich countries; intensified geochemical and geological mapping of the world; and national and international monitoring groups to warn of impending critical shortages and to recommend remedies. They state that: "Above all, new discovery is required that, together with technological innovation, will develop reserves of mineral resources at an exponential rate until population control and relatively constant or decreasing per capita demand can be achieved—both inevitable requirements on our finite earth." They add: "if the present divisiveness of the world persists . . . nations will need to buffer their economies against external control of vital resources or else exploit the scarcities of others in those commodities that they have in exportable surplus. It would seem better for all concerned to promote policies of co-existence and co-operation." [11] If such policies are not pursued, the poor countries, whose mineral resources are less developed, may be tempted ultimately to hold the rich countries to ransom. The largest reserves of some key minerals are in their hands: tin in Malaysia and Thailand; tungsten in China; nickel in Cuba and New Caledonia; iron in South America; copper in Chile, Zaire and Zambia; cobalt in the Republic of Congo and Zambia; and aluminum in Guinea and Jamaica.[12] A further great question mark, however, hangs over the whole problem of minerals: the provision of energy. Aluminum requires twenty times more energy to extract from ore than does iron. Fifteen million watt-hours of energy are required to mine one ton of copper; and the amount required will be far greater when lower grade ores have to be used.

Energy is perhaps the major key to the solution of the technological problems of development. If the means of producing and distributing inexhaustible supplies of energy could be found, the technological solutions to the crises of food production and mineral depletion might be in sight.

At present 40 percent of the energy used in the world is derived from coal, oil, gas, wood or dung directly consumed in machines or other ways.[13] The rest is derived from electricity, which in its turn is produced mainly from coal, oil and natural gas. The world's consumption of total energy is doubling every 20 years, and of electricity every 10 years. By the year 2000, 6 times as much electricity may be needed by the 6–7 billion people who will probably then be inhabiting the planet as that which is being used by 3.8 billion people today. If a really significant rise in the standard of living of the poor countries were to take place in the next 30 years, the figure would be bigger still. "Obviously, the present rate of increase cannot continue for a very long time; electricity production doubling every 10 years for seven centuries would require, according to Einstein's law, the annihilation of the whole earth, its entire mass being converted into energy." [14]

The rich countries account for over 80 percent of the world's total consumption; and the United States for half the rich countries consumption.[15] The development of the poor countries will therefore require that they should consume a greater proportion of the world's total, unless certain technological breakthroughs occur which we shall discuss below; and this may require that the rich countries slow down their rate of increased consumption, or even reduce their total consumption below present levels.

The fossil fuels, like the minerals, are being irrevocably depleted. Estimates of the rates of exhaustion vary. The consensus of opinion seems to be that petroleum might last another thirty to eighty years[16] —peak production may well have been reached by the year 2000—and coal for one to three centuries. For the next thirty years, petroleum and coal could meet the major needs of the planet at present rates of consumption. But the problem of the location of supplies is now also worrying the rich countries. Their main source of energy has hitherto been coal, which lies under their own soil. For economic reasons, however, they have in recent years been increasingly switching from coal to oil and natural gas: in 1970 coal provided less than 40 percent of world energy needs, oil nearly 40 percent, and gas the balance. Most of the world's oil, however, is in the developing countries—the Middle East, North Africa, Venezuela, Nigeria and Indonesia. Western Europe and Japan are almost entirely dependent on these sources; the United States is now importing nearly 30 percent of its oil; and from 1979 will be importing very large quantities of Siberian natural gas from the Soviet Union under a trade agreement of 1972. For reasons discussed in Chapter 14, the rich countries are increasingly reluctant to rely on the poor countries for this vital commodity.

Economic and political pressures are therefore impelling the rich countries to turn to atomic energy as a major source of energy. This introduces a completely new factor into the economy of the world, a far more revolutionary factor, even, than the change from burning wood, peat and dung to burning coal and oil. It involves drawing on the primal energy of the universe, "bringing down to earth the powers which would never have permitted any kind of organic life to develop on the planet, had not millennia been spent in building up protective mechanisms—the oceans, the first creations of oxygen and ozone, the breathing out of the all-encompassing atmosphere by the earth's growing cover of green plants." [17] Three million times more heat is generated by the atomic fission of any mass of uranium than by the combustion of the same mass of coal.[18]

The development of nuclear fission from uranium was expanded in the fifties by the United States, the Soviet Union, Britain, France and Canada. By 1972, seventy-three nuclear power reactors had been constructed in thirteen non-Communist countries, including two in the developing world, India and Pakistan.[19] Even in the rich countries, however, they were producing only a fraction of the total energy consumed. For the fissionable proportion of any given quantity of the high-grade uranium which they require is very small, less than 1 percent; and the world's deposits of this "rich" uranium are limited. The expansion of nuclear power therefore now depends on the development of a new type of "breeder" reactor, which will breed plutonium (a manmade mineral) for the existing reactors from low-grade uranium, which is in virtually limitless supply, using 70 to 80 percent of the ore. The process has hitherto been technically difficult and expensive. Britain and the Soviet Union, with other countries further behind, are, however, now developing prototypes of breeder reactors which may prove commercially attractive. "The breeder reactor should make it possible for nuclear fission to supply the world's energy needs for the next millennium." [20] The Atomic Energy authorities in Britain and the United States estimate that by 1980, 15 percent of the world's energy will be supplied by nuclear power and, by the year 2000, perhaps 50 percent. "The United States Government has recently announced that intensive development of the fast breeder is now national policy." [21] West Germany, France and Italy are planning to develop their breeder reactors jointly.[22]

The combustion of coal and oil are polluting the atmosphere in the cities of the world with toxic substances—sulfur dioxide and carbon monoxide—and oil leakages from tankers are polluting the oceans. Most of the rich countries are beginning to take action to bring this fossil fuel pollution under control, though it may be some time before their measures are effective. Fission nuclear power is, by comparison, "clean," but it produces radioactive wastes which must be sealed up and stored in the earth. It may take several thousand years for these wastes to disintegrate. At present the quantities of this waste are quite small; but Dr. Alvin Weinberg, a world expert on nuclear energy, has said that on the basis of current projections, 24,000 breeder reactors would be required to provide the power which the world would need in 1990; and that two of these would be "used up" each day, so that mountains of radioactive waste would be accumulating. Another feature of the breeder reactor is that it can easily be switched over to the manufacture of thermonuclear bombs, though complex preparation is needed.[23] There are also the dangers of accidental leakage of radioactive material if the reactor's cooling system should break down.

In most major industrial concerns, developing in a competitive race for commercial profit and/or national prestige, there is a built-in temptation to brush aside the effects on human health and the natural environment, relying on technology to deal with such subsidiary problems. In the case of nuclear-fission energy, however, these problems are of an entirely new kind. The Test Ban Treaty of 1963 forbade the aboveground testing of nuclear weapons because it was then realized that the relatively small amounts of radioactive material released into the atmosphere might be contributing to the incidence of cancer and leukemia. Radioactivity is now known for certain to have long-term genetic effects.[24] This knowledge recently prompted the United States Government to reduce the federal standards concerning exposure of citizens to radioactive emissions by 100 percent. The nuclear power industry has pioneered in anticipating environmental hazards and in taking precautionary measures; but since the results of an accident could be lethal on an unprecedented scale, unprecedented control measures for this industry may be necessary. "At the very least an international authority of unimpeachable scientific integrity must be the licensing body for reactor sales," say two leading authorities on the environment.[25] Dr. Alvin Weinberg believes that nuclear power stations should be confined "to a relatively small number of what I call nuclear parks," segregated from densely inhabited areas.[26] The case for the international management of this tremendous force, which, if fully developed, could transform or destroy rich and poor countries alike, would seem to be strong.

An even more dramatic development is now on the horizon: the generation of electricity by nuclear fusion: the reproduction on the earth of the process of reconversion of hydrogen atoms into helium which is going on all the time in the sun. The fusion reactor's main fuel would be deuterium, which is found in water. The technical problems, in particular that of how to control the generation of heat of the order of 100 million degrees centigrade, may be solved by the end of the next decade. The research is being carried out, at the cost of some \$120 million, by the major rich countries, working in close collaboration, and with the Soviet Union taking the lead. "Fusion energy is kind to the ecosystem. The fusion process does not result in radioactive ashes and produces minimum radiation." Its fuel is derived from the inexhaustible and costless waters of the oceans, and it would have no military potential.[27] If fusion reactors prove to be technically feasible, therefore, it would seem highly desirable to reach international agreement to replace fission by fusion energy. Although the fusion reactors are likely to be cheap to operate, they will be very expensive to build. "Because of the magnitude of the venture there is no possibility of fusion energy becoming the domain or province of one or two or three large companies. . . . Here is an area which could bring about a new intensity of international cooperation," says a Californian physicist. "There's every chance that fusion energy production will be one of the very few ventures in which we can engage without international competitiveness," because "it means that everyone would have the means to achieve wealth, namely, unlimited energy resources. . . . It could be the most revolutionary thing that has happened in a thousand years." [28]

Other possible means of gaining energy which are now being explored are to draw on the heat inside the earth and to harness the rays of the sun. Small experiments in geothermic energy are being carried out in a few countries. The technology of tapping solar energy is understood, but it offers little prospect of providing a large-scale source of electric power. Its potential use would seem to be as a sort of intermediate technology, to provide simple installations, which could be constructed by local labor, dispersed over the countryside in developing countries, where the sun shines strongly most of the time. A long-term possibility, which is being studied in the United States, is that of beaming solar power to the earth from satellites in space.[29] If this becomes feasible, it would no doubt also call for international cooperation, if not international management.

References

1. *Sinews for Survival: A Report on the Management of Natural Resources to the Secretary of State for the Environment* [of the British Government], February 1972 (London: Her Majesty's Stationery Office, 1972), p. 27.

2. Barbara Ward and René Dubos, *Only One Earth: The Care and Maintenance of a Small Planet* (Middlesex, England: Penguin Books, Ltd., 1972), p. 179.

3. Harrison Brown, "Human Material Production as a Process in the Biosphere," in *Scientific American,* September 1970, pp. 194–209.

4. Donella H. Meadows, Dennis L. Meadows, Jørgen Randers and William W. Behrens III, *The Limits to Growth* (New York: Universe Books, 1972), Table, pp. 56–59.

5. Harrison Brown, *op. cit.*

6. *The Weekly Guardian* (London), October 21, 1972.

7. See, for example, "A Blueprint for Survival," in *The Ecologist* (Richmond, Surrey, England), Vol. 2, No. 1, January 1972, Table on p. 7; and Paul R. Ehrlich

and Anne H. Ehrlich, *Population, Resources Environment: Issues in Human Ecology,* San Francisco, California: W. H. Freeman & Company, 1972 (second edition), p. 71.

8. *Sinews for Survival, op. cit.,* p. 27.

9. Barbara Ward and René Dubos, *op. cit.,* pp. 179–83.

10. *Ibid.,* p. 181.

11. United States National Academy of Sciences-National Research Council, *Resources and Man* (San Francisco, California: W. H. Freeman & Company, 1969), pp. 128–33.

12. Meadows *et al., op. cit.,* pp. 56–59.

13. Chauncy Starr, "Energy and Power," in *Scientific American,* September 1971, Vol. 224, No. 3, p. 43.

14. Francis Perrin, "Recent Advances in Energy Systems," in *Managing the Planet,* ed. Peter Albertson and Margery Barnet (Englewood Cliffs, N.J.: Prentice-Hall, Inc., 1972), p. 130.

15. From: *World Energy Supplies, 1966–9* (New York: United Nations, November 1971).

16. Fred H. Singer, "Human Energy as a Process in the Biosphere," in *Scientific American,* September 1970, pp. 176–78; and Barbara Ward and René Dubos *op. cit.* p. 184.

17. Barbara Ward and René Dubos, *op. cit.,* p. 186.

18. Francis Perrin, *op. cit.,* p. 134.

19. Information from the British Atomic Energy Authority.

20. *British Atomic Energy Authority Bulletin* No. 4, 1970, and *The Economist* (London), February 29, 1971.

21. Chauncy Starr, *op. cit.,* p. 44.

22. "Energy in Europe," *The Times* (London), Special Report, July 5, 1972.

23. Information received from the Parliamentary Group for World Government, House of Commons, London.

24. Information received from Dr. Klaus-Rüdiger Trott, Cancer Research Expert, Munich University.

25. Barbara Ward and René Dubos, *op. cit.,* p. 194.

26. "Must the World Take a Power Cut," in *The Observer* (London), March 12, 1972.

27. Information received from the Atomic Energy Agency, London, and Center for the Study of Democratic Institutions, Santa Barbara, California, *Center Report,* Vol. 5, No. 4, October 1972, pp. 8–9.

28. *Ibid.*

29. *The Observer* (London), September 3, 1972.

nineteen

SHARING THE OCEAN'S RESOURCES

It is suddenly being realized that the food resources, minerals and fossil fuels in the oceans, which cover 70 percent of the earth's surface, may be of real importance in filling the growing gap between world needs and world supplies. The problem of how these resources should be exploited, husbanded, shared and kept free from pollution is therefore now becoming urgent. Hitherto the seas have been more or less a free-for-all, and clashes of interest in the development of their resources, such as the recent British-Icelandic "cod war," have not arisen on any major scale. Now, however, the need for the systematic development of their resources, combined with the invention of highly sophisticated technology for doing so, has produced an entirely new situation.

First, we must note the distinction between the continental margin, the seabed which slopes down from the surface land to the deep ocean, and the deep ocean floor. The continental margin is divided by geologists into three zones: the continental shelf, defined in international law as extending to a depth of two hundred meters (see below); the continental slope; and the continental rise. The continental margin occupies a fifth of the whole area of the oceans.

The oil which is at present being extracted from the oceans lies under the continental shelf. Further major resources of oil and natural gas are believed to lie under the continental slope and rise. The whole of the North Sea, where oil and gas have recently been discovered, consists of continental margin. Geologists believe that little or no oil exists under the deep ocean floor—though drilling there has begun. On the other hand, it is on the ocean floor that the mineral nodules lie, and the technology for dredging them up is being rapidly developed. The United States corporation "Deep Sea Ventures," which has developed an air-lift hydraulic system, has promised its stockholders that it will be dredging up a million tons of nodules by 1974.[1] The fish, which swim in the deep seas and in the shallower margins, are being overhunted by certain nations, as we have seen in Chapter 17; and some form of aquaculture is now needed to safeguard and breed stocks. It has been suggested that one way of doing this could be by sinking a nuclear reactor onto the ocean floor; its heat would stir up the seas and eventually increase the primary food on which the fish feed.[2]

It is technically possible for individual states or individual companies to exploit the oil and dredge up the minerals in the oceans; although if the situation remains a free-for-all there might well be a scramble to grab these resources, in which the poor countries and countries with little or no sea coasts would be the inevitable losers. Aquaculture, however, would almost certainly be impossible except on an international basis; and pollution control will also require international action.

International law regarding the rights of nations to the resources of the oceans is ill-defined. As regards surface waters, international law developed during the past three and a half centuries has asserted the doctrine of the freedom of the seas; and three miles—the distance that a cannon ball could be fired—became established as the limit for "territorial waters." Some states with a limited maritime access, like Russia, however, claimed twelve miles; and recently these claims have been greatly extended: by Iceland to fifty miles; by Canada to one hundred miles (to protect her waters from the oil spills of foreign tankers); and by some Latin American states to two hundred miles (to protect "their" fish from the predatory activities of the rich countries).

The situation with regard to the continental margin is only slightly less ambiguous. A Geneva Convention of 1958 recognized coastal states' sovereignty over the continental shelf to a depth of two hundred meters or beyond "where the depth of the super-adjacent waters admits of the exploitation of natural resources." Taking advantage of this vague phrase, the countries with coastlines on the North Sea have divided the bed of this sea among themselves and are now rapidly exploiting its oil and gas. "This exploitability criterion," writes an international lawyer, "has proved to be the starting point for an almost unlimited outward and downward expansion of exclusive continental-shelf claims and for the virtual elimination of the concept of the continental shelf as a legally meaningful limitation of national sovereign rights." [3] The twenty-nine landlocked states, and the fifty or so states which have only small coastal footholds, view with increasing misgiving this creeping extension into the oceans of the sovereignty of the maritime nations.

Such was the situation when, on December 17, 1970, the General Assembly of the United Nations passed what may prove to be a historic Declaration. The seabed and its resources were declared to be "the common heritage of mankind," and "no state should claim sovereign rights over any part thereof." "All activities regarding the exploration and exploitation of the resources of the area should be governed by an international regime to be established . . . for the benefit of mankind as a whole, taking into particular consideration the interests and needs of the developing countries." The Declaration was passed without a dissenting vote, although fourteen states, most of them Communist, abstained.

The interpretation of this Declaration raises a number of questions. Should the common heritage be regarded as stretching from coast to coast, or should the current concept that coastal states have a "right" to sovereignty over surface territorial waters and over some part of the continental shelf be retained, and if so, what should be the agreed limits of these waters be—twelve miles wide and two hundred meters deep, or more? Should the potentially oil-rich continental slope and rise be included in the zone of national or of international sovereignty? What should be the structure, functions and powers of the international regime? It is generally accepted by governments that it would issue licenses, either to states or to corporations, for exploitation in the seas, against the payment of royalties which would be internationally distributed, with special regard for the needs of the poor countries.

These matters will be discussed at a United Nations conference on the law of the sea in 1974. The United States Government, supported by that of Britain, has proposed that the coastal states should act as trustees for the international community in the development of the continental slope and rise. They would receive a share of the international revenue accruing, which they would also have the right to tax. This plan has been described by members of the British House of Lords, when debating the subject, as "robbery from the common heritage of mankind," or "ocean colonialism." [4] For the exploitation of the deep seas beyond the continental margin, the British Government has proposed a "grid" system, under which all states would have blocks of the ocean bed assigned to them by the international regime. This proposal was described in the House of Lords as "international bingo," since the quotas of blocks would be assigned before their resources were explored. It has also been pointed out that the proposal "maximizes the bargaining power of a small number of technically qualified companies, for whose services 130-odd administering governments would be obliged desperately to compete. If the international authority allocated the blocks direct, on the other hand, the companies themselves will be competing with each other for blocks, so the bargaining position would be exactly reversed." [5]

The idea of turning three-quarters of the earth's surface, with all its largely unexplored resources, into "the common heritage of mankind" has profound implications. The resources of the sea cannot in the long run be separated from those of the soil. How will international management of the oil, the fish, the minerals, the pollution of the sea mesh in with national management by some one hundred forty states of the resources of the other quarter of the globe? "The common heritage of mankind is a creeping concept." [6] It opens the way to a new kind of legal order, to be established in an area where no national sovereignty or property has ever existed. The new approach will involve asking not "Who owns this property?" but "Who is to benefit from this asset? What purpose does its development serve?" Different kinds of ownership could be incorporated within the overall plan for the common management in the common interest. The "international regime" provided for in the United Nations Resolution may have to move away from the standard structure, that of a confederation of the sovereign nation states, and develop as a new kind of political organism, for which the supranational European Community may provide a model.[7] To be effective, the Oceanic Community will have to have powers to carry out research, exploitation and management activities; to employ and license operators; to make and enforce "the law of the sea," perhaps with the aid of observation satellites; and to raise its own taxes, which might be levied on the basis of the GNP of participating nations. A suggested statute for the Ocean Regime, put forward by the Center for Democratic Studies at Santa Barbara, California, includes the proposal that scientific and professional interests should be directly represented in the governing maritime assembly. The voices of those best qualified to speak in the common interest would thus be heard together with those representing national interests.[8]

"The principle that ocean environment and ocean resources are the common heritage of mankind is the basis for a new theory of development," writes the author of the suggested statute. "It abolishes the principle of donor and recipient and substitutes for it the idea of rightful and equitable sharing among all nations of what belongs to them in common." [9]

Lord Wilberforce, a leading British lawyer, has suggested that the phrase "the common heritage of mankind" "can be used as a legal concept towards solving the otherwise intractable problems of the sea—environment, exploitation, research. It seems to be a different concept from saying that the sea is *res nullius,* or *res communis.* It carries the idea, not only that all people (I prefer this to all States) have a right to enjoy its benefits, but that there is a common duty to preserve and cultivate its resources for everyone's benefit. This enables us to bring exploitation and conservation together and starts at the international (i.e., the world) rather than the national end." [10] It also involves departing from the modern notion of property as a personal right—which even in municipal law is beginning to fade; for example, in many Western countries a person cannot build a house, or even make structural alterations to an existing house, without getting "planning permission" from the local authorities. It reintroduces, in a modern secular form, the premodern idea of property as a sacred trust for the community, which we discussed in Chapter 2.

If this new legal concept of property is developed for the objects in the oceans, can it be withheld permanently from the objects in or on the land?

References

1. United Nations General Assembly Committee on the Peaceful Uses of the Seabed and the Ocean Floor Beyond the Limits of National Jurisdiction, A/AC 138/36 of May 28, 1971, pp. 45–46; Hansard, Parliamentary Debates, House of Lords, Vol. 313, No. 27, p. 134 and p. 182.

2. *The Sunday Times* (London), June 18, 1972.

3. Wolfgang Friedmann, *The Future of the Oceans* (New York: Braziller, 1971), p. 37.

4. Hansard, *op. cit.,* p. 137.

5. Evan Luard in *The Times* (London), July 17, 1972.

6. Elisabeth Mann Borgese, "The World Community," in *The Center Magazine* (Santa Barbara, California: The Center for the Study of Democratic Institutions), Vol. 4, No. 5, September–October 1971, p. 11.

7. Jean-Pierre Lévy, *L'Ordre Internationale de Development des Fonds Marin.* (Paris: Editions A. Pedone, 1971), pp. 17–28.

8. Elisabeth Mann Borgese, *The Ocean Regime* (Santa Barbara, California: The Center for the Study of Democratic Institutions, 1968).

9. Elisabeth Mann Borgese, "The World Community," *op. cit.,* p. 11.

10. In a letter to the author dated December 18, 1972.

twenty

THE ECOLOGICAL CHALLENGE

During the sixties scientists and citizens in the rich countries began to be worried about the way in which economic growth is disturbing the planet's ecosphere. Erosion and salinization have destroyed some five hundred million hectares of arable land, and two-thirds of the world's forests have been lost to production.[1] Plants, and the animals which feed on them, are being poisoned by pesticides—an estimated billion pounds of DDT have been dumped into the environment.[2] Increasing dependence on fewer crop strains is destroying nature's gene pool. The rivers and lakes are being polluted by detergents, pesticides, sewage, factory wastes and hot water from the coolers of power plants (nuclear plants require 50 percent as much cooling water as fossil fuel plants). The oceans, described in a United Nations report as "the world's sinks," are likewise being polluted by the effluents from the rivers and the air, and by the direct dumping of oil and toxic matter in them. The air is being poisoned by the toxic emissions from the burning of fossil fuels in automobiles, airplanes and factories. Each year some two hundred fifty thousand different chemicals are projected into the atmosphere; their genetic effects are unknown: they could produce genetic catastrophe.[3] The delicate balance of nature is being upset to the point where there could be a breakdown. Symptoms of ecospheric disease are the facts that fish and plants have been killed off in many lakes, rivers and parts of the seas; that certain species of birds which eat the insects which eat the crops are dying out; that some of the pests are becoming resistant to pesticides; that the incidence of lung disease is increasing among the inhabitants of smog-filled cities; and so on. One possible longer-term result of pollution may be the alteration of the climate. The carbon dioxide in the air produced by the combustion of coal and oil has increased 10 percent during the past century, and, at present rates of consumption, could rise to 25 percent by the year 2000.⁴ This could warm up the planetary temperature to the point where the polar ice caps might melt and cause the oceans to rise and flood low-lying coastal areas. Another potential danger lies in the increasing dependence on inorganic fertilizers to produce the world's food. "It has been predicted that in 25 to 50 years the ultimate crisis in agriculture will occur in the United States. Either the fertility of the soil will drop precipitously, because inorganic fertilizers will be withheld, throwing the nation into a food crisis, or the amounts of inorganic nitrates and phosphates applied to the land will be so large as to cause an insoluble water pollution problem." ⁵ A third longerterm danger, to which we have already alluded, is that of massive exposure of living things to radioactive material resulting from the development of nuclear power stations. These are merely some examples of the looming ecological crisis. Man's global ecological impact is said to be doubling every fourteen years; so he may expect fourteen years' warning of impending disaster.⁶

Apart from soil erosion, salinization and deforestation, which are serious problems in the developing world, the environmental crisis is essentially a product of the rich countries' technology. Fifty percent of the world's pollution stems from the United States, which led the world in the technological explosion which has occurred since 1945. This explosion has in its turn been stimulated by the new idea of deliberately promoting economic growth through managing the economy (see Chapter 3).

For a time the analytical nature of the scientific method screened the impending crisis. The experts in each subject, the technologists on each project, tend to work in isolation from each other: it would be beyond the capacity of the human brain to be a specialist in all the different branches of science and technology which have proliferated in the last twenty-five years. The private-enterprise system has encouraged individual inventiveness; but it has also fostered the tendency to "go it alone." Each company wants to monopolize its own inventions, and to exploit them to the full for the sake of the accruing profits. The impact of his products on other aspects of life, for example, the impact of detergents on the organisms in rivers, is not the manufacturer's concern. Property is a commodity to which individuals have a "right" of private exploitation.

Suddenly, in the late sixties, awareness of the ecological crisis erupted into the public consciousness of the rich countries—stimulated by professional ecologists, who are now attempting to look scientifically at the ecosphere as an organic unit of interrelated parts.

The computer is coming to their aid by making it possible, for the first time, to correlate the vast amount of factual information produced by the many branches of science. It has also been inspired by a growing *feeling* about the importance of preserving "the quality of life" in nature. The conservation movement has coincided with a growing interest in Oriental religions, such as Chinese Taoism and Japanese Zen Buddhism, whose keynote is the inherent harmony between man and nature.

Spurred on by the ecologists, the governments of the rich countries are now beginning to take action on a national basis to deal with pollution. A number of European countries have set up Ministries of the Environment, and the United States has established an Environmental Agency and a Council on Environmental Quality, which called for an expenditure of $105 billion between 1970 and 1975 (of which 42 percent would be paid by industry) for a partial cleanup of American air, water and solid-waste pollution.[7] Antipollution legislation is on the national statute books.

The statesmen are also recognizing that pollution does not observe national frontiers. "We know that we must act as one world in restoring the world's environment, before pollution of the seas and the skies overwhelms every nation," said President Nixon in his second Foreign Policy message to Congress in 1970. This recognition led to the convening of the first United Nations Conference on the Human Environment in Stockholm in June 1972. The conference was attended by representatives of 114 states of the Western world and the developing countries, including China. (It was boycotted by the Soviet Union and most of the Communist countries of Eastern Europe because East Germany was not invited.)

The Conference produced an impressive Declaration of Principles, and a 109-point Action Plan. The Principles affirm the regional or global nature of most environmental problems, and the need for "rational planning." The principle of the sovereign right of states to exploit their own resources is asserted, but with the significant rider that they have the responsibility to ensure that their activities do not damage the environment of other states. Many of the poor countries defended their environmental sovereignty as passionately as did the rich countries. One of the main protagonists of national sovereignty was China, which emerged more definitely than at UNCTAD III as a spokesman for the poor countries, presenting its own environmental policies as a model—though its claim was weakened by its concern to maintain its status as a nuclear power in the face of the Conference's general condemnation of nuclear weapons and tests. Another such country was Brazil, which frustrated a scheme for the international monitoring of forest conservation—some ecologists attacked its plans for exploiting its forests as "environmental Hiroshima." [8] The nations of the world were not yet prepared to consider means for the international enforcement of the Environmental Principles which the Conference laid down.

The recommendations of the Action Plan included a ten-year moritorium on whale hunting; a world-wide network of at least 110 atmospheric monitoring stations; a special international fund to finance housing and other forms of "human settlement" in the developing countries; a global network of national and regional institutes for genetic resource conservation; an international Referral Service to provide environmental information; and an international convention to forbid the dumping of toxic matters in the oceans. The whaling moratorium would at present affect primarily the Soviet Union and Japan, whose huge modern whalers catch 80 percent of the kill—some 40,000 whales a year; but on a long-term basis the breeding and conservation of whales is a matter of interest to the poor countries, since whale meat could help to meet their protein needs. The proposal was, however, subsequently rejected by the International Whaling Commission, a body composed of the whaling nations; it merely agreed to set quotas for some species. In November 1972, 57 states signed a convention to forbid the dumping of poisonous matter in the oceans; but discussion of methods of enforcing the convention was deferred until 1973.

The Conference proposed the establishment of a United Nations Environmental Secretariat, with a budget of one hundred million dollars for five years, to promote action on its recommendations. The General Assembly of the United Nations, which in December 1972 endorsed all the Conference's recommendations, decided that this body should be located in Nairobi—the first United Nations organ to be established in a developing country.

The poor countries had initially regarded the Conference with great suspicion, as a plot of the rich countries to frustrate their development by crying "pollution." They therefore took the opportunity to turn this idea around and to argue that their underdevelopment is itself a form of planetary pollution. A report prepared for the Conference by a group of experts drawn equally from the rich and the poor countries stated: "Not merely the quality of life, but life itself, is endangered by poor water, housing, sanitation and nutrition, by disease and sickness and natural disasters. These are problems, no less than those of industrial pollution, that clamour for attention in the context of the concern with the human environment." So, this time on environmental grounds, the poor countries reiterated their demands for more aid, for stable prices for their exports of primary products and for the transfer of technology free of charge—which the Western countries rejected.[9] They agreed that "environmental considerations should be incorporated into national development plans, so as to avoid the mistakes made by the industrialized nations, and thereby, to enhance the quality of life of their peoples." But they urged that the rich countries must not allow their own antipollution measures to distort their aid policies, for example, by refusing to import goods from the poor countries which might be polluted, or limiting imports of goods which might be recycled. They demanded that in cases, for example, such as the rejection by American importers of Peruvian fish contaminated by chemicals injected into the sea by the United States, the exporters should be compensated; and that the rich countries should pay the cost of adding antipollution equipment to their industrial aid (the "principle of additionality"). The rich countries objected.[10]

This clash of interest over the very nature of "pollution" dramatized the nature of the gulf between the rich and the poor countries: one group of countries disturbing the delicate balance of the ecosphere by overconsumption and the other by underconsumption. It began to focus the need to shift away from the concept of "bridging the gulf between the haves and have-nots" towards the concept of an equitable sharing among all planetary citizens of the common planetary resources. Attempts made by some of the rich countries to brush aside the issue of underdevelopment as irrelevant to pollution were foiled.

On the face of it, the poor countries did not gain much from the Stockholm Conference. The scene seems to be set for the rich countries to go ahead with cleaning up their own pollution, while refusing to make any real effort to combat the other kind of pollution—underdevelopment—and perhaps even allowing their antipollution measures to cramp the poor countries' efforts.

This was the first international conference of its kind to be directly influenced by informed nonofficial opinion. The presence, inside and outside the conference halls, of two thousand journalists, the representatives of some four hundred fifty nongovernmental bodies and a host of individual scientists and concerned young people made a real impact on the proceedings. "The criticism was so well-informed that one diplomat spoke of the uncomfortable realization, for an official, that many of the nonofficial experts present were better informed than those advising the governments." [11] This experience is a pointer to the need to ensure, in the structure of international organizations concerned with the management of the planet, that some special official representation is given to concerned nongovernmental groups, such as scientists and religious bodies (see Chapter 21).

One of the significant results of the Conference was the emergence into the public arena of the theme "to grow or not to grow." The large majority agreed with Mr. McNamara, President of the World Bank, that "the only way to tackle environmental squalor is to create more wealth with which to do it." M. Sicco Mansholt, the Chairman of the Commission of the European Community, challenged this attitude, arguing that the elimination of industrial pollution requires the rich countries to stabilize or reduce their growth rates, while continuing to help the poor countries to develop.[12] We shall return to this subject in Chapter 21.

Despite the limited nature of its achievements, the Conference injected a new perspective into the international scene. The concept that "the care and maintenance of a small planet" through "rational planning" is a common human concern was launched into the collective consciousness. Maurice Strong, the Secretary-General of the Conference and the Director of the new Environmental Secretariat, has suggested that perhaps the most important achievement of the Conference is the assertion that pollution travelling from one country to another is an "invasion," implying that the offender is guilty of "aggression." [13] This may open up a new field of international law, and provide the lead-in for the crucial missing factor—enforcement measures.

The quesion of what kind of environment the global planners should plan for has barely begun to be asked. This question is particularly vital for the poor countries, which wish to take their place as technologically developed countries in an unpolluted planet. The ecological crisis is thus pointing the way towards the need for a model for global technological development in harmony with nature, and for common action to create this model.

References

1. The United Nations, *The Human Environment: New Challenge for the United Nations*. United Nations pamphlet OPI/433-02726, February 1971, p. 4.

2. *Ibid.*, p. 5.

3. Dr. Jack Shubert, Professor of Radiation Chemistry, University of Pittsburgh, at the Stockholm Conference. *The Times* (London), June 14, 1972.

4. The United Nations, *The Human Environment, op. cit.*, p. 4.

5. Paul R. Ehrlich and Anne H. Ehrlich, *Population, Resources, Environment: Issues in Human Ecology*, Second Edition (San Francisco, California: W. H. Freeman & Company, 1972), p. 232.

6. Paul Ehrlich and John Holdern, in *The Times* (London), June 27, 1972.

7. *Second Annual Report of the Council on Environmental Quality* (Washington, D.C.: U.S. Government Printing Office, 1971), pp. 110–11.

8. *The Observer* (London), June 11, 1972.

9. *The Times* (London), June 15, 1972.

10. *The Observer* (London), June 11, 1972.
11. *Vista, The Magazine of the United Nations Association of the USA*, September–October 1972, p. 15.
12. *The Observer* (London), June 11, 1972.
13. Edward P. Morgan, "Stockholm, the Clean (but Impossible) Dream," in *Foreign Policy* (New York: National Affairs Council), No. 8, Fall 1972.

twenty-one

TOWARD WORLD COMMUNITY

The planet is going through a crisis of transformation. The premodern societies are evolving into modern society, and modern society may itself be a transition to world community. The great ideas on which modern society is grounded—the ideas of science and of the rights of man—imply progress toward a better life for men on this earth. In their internal affairs the rich countries are putting these ideas into practice through such policies and institutions as constitutional government, fair legal systems, public ownership of public utilities and productive enterprises, economic planning, the management of economic factors and the welfare state—some within the context of multiparty political democracy, others in the context of a one-party Communist state. In all of them the idea that people should participate actively in the economic and political processes is gaining ground. And in developing these policies, the rich countries are increasingly cooperating with each other in a host of international institutions. On the negative side of the balance, the secular materialism of the rich countries has produced immense problems of overconsumption, pollution and psychological alienation; while in international relations, attitudes of national prestige and fear have stimulated the most sinister arms race in history.

The monumental problems of the poor countries arise from the determination to enter into the modern phase of development which the rich countries have already reached. These interconnected problems of population explosion, land tenure, urbanization, unemployment, elitism, education, health, government and defense, add up to a crisis situation. Unless urgent and massive measures are taken to solve them, they may produce famine, violence and chaos on a scale which could disrupt the whole planet. U Thant, the late Lester Pearson, Robert McNamara and Norman Borlaug are a few of those who have issued most solemn warnings to the governments of the world.

Within the poor countries, solutions to these problems are increasingly being sought in terms of "integrated development," involving land reform, planning, public ownership, community development and welfare services. While these measures are essentially modelled on the systems which the rich countries are developing, in certain fields, such as functional education and preventive medicine, the poor countries may soon be providing models for the rich. In most of these countries, however, with the major exception of China, the implementation of these policies is only in its first stages; and in some, political revolution may be necessary before they can be launched.

As rich and poor countries alike struggle to solve their problems in terms of the dynamic process of industrial development, the absolute gulf between them inexorably widens. We have seen how the rich countries have accepted the principle that they must do something to bridge the gulf, but that the measures taken have been inadequate in relation to the magnitude of the problems, and are sometimes counterproductive. The help has been given in the spirit of the rich man's sense of duty to give charity to the poor, or else in such a way as in fact to promote the rich countries' own interests. Finally, we have seen that within the past decade public awareness of certain basic *global* problems has emerged: the problems of world food supplies in relation to the exploding population; of the depletion of the irreplaceable resources of minerals and fossil fuels; of the development of atomic energy; of the exploitation of the resources of the oceans; and of the global effects of pollution.

The emergence of these global problems is prompting entirely new attempts to make models (the concept of a "model," with its Platonic implications, has come into current use in the past decade) of the overall global situation, and to project these models into the future, in order to assess what should be done on a global scale to prevent disasters and to solve the problems. The first of these models was commissioned by the "Club of Rome," an *ad hoc* group of thirty distinguished men from ten countries, founded in 1968 by Aurelio Peccei, Vice-President of Olivetti and Fiat, and Sir Alexander King, Director-General for Scientific Affairs of OECD. A group of experts at MIT, led by Jay Forrester and Dennis Meadows, fed "six major variables and 90 equations with innumerable feedback loops" into a computer. "The variables were: world population; food required by that increasing population; the agricultural potential to provide the food; industrial and economic growth; depletion of raw materials, and pollution." [1] * According to Sir Alexander King, "The kind of model the human brain can envisage doesn't carry more than about three variables at a time, and therefore our model was infinitely more complicated than anything the human brain can deal with." The computer produced the conclusion that, in Sir Alexander's words, "the whole thing would come to a halt somewhere in the middle of the next century. The striking thing is that no matter what maxima and minima one took in the various assumptions—optimistic and pessimistic—the results seemed to be the same. For example, if one held down population, the per capita increase in demands would lead to depletion of raw materials and pollution saturation. Forrester and Meadows were so upset by these results that they played about in every possible way to try to get an equilibrium and not a collapse." The variables did not include armaments. Sir Alexander's guess is that "if there were real disarmament, the calculations might give us another twenty or thirty years. This might be critical." [2]

The computer's findings were published in March 1972 in a small book called *The Limits to Growth*.[3] It made an immediate impact around the world, and aroused violent controversy among economists and businessmen. Its critics dispute the selection of the material fed into the computer (the Science Policy Research Unit at Sussex University in England is publishing a large volume on this),[4] and in particular, the exclusion, on the plus side, of the exponential growth of technology. But even the severest critics cannot deny the fact that this first attempt to put together in a model all the major problems facing the human race (except for armaments) has revealed a looming crisis. The controversy is therefore now beginning to center around the questions: should growth be "limited"—should mankind aim at a zero growth rate or a steady state world economy; or should growth continue, but in a managed and planned form? According to Professor Zbigniew Brzezinski of Columbia University, "The alternative to zero growth is not massive, undirected growth, but planned, purposeful growth. We do need to define for ourselves more precisely what kind of a society we wish to build, in which direction we wish the world to head, and what ecological concerns humanity shares in common. The answer to that will be provided, in very large measure, by further economic and scientific growth, but growth geared to more deliberately defined obectives than has been the case in the past." [5] In either case, the implications are revolutionary—as revolutionary, says Sir Alexander, "as the Communist Manifesto was. It's leading towards a

* Quotations from references 1, 2, 6, 7, 8—Alexander King, "The Totality of the World *Problematique* Must Now Be Addressed"—are reprinted by permission of the Center for the Study of Democratic Institutions, Santa Barbara, California.

post-capitalist, post-Marxist, post-liberal kind of society, all of which raises many and perhaps the most urgent questions in the world today." [6]

The revolutionary implications will be clearer when other studies, which the MIT study has provoked, are completed. By October 1972 about twenty had been set in hand in different parts of the world. One consists of a model being constructed in Argentina to examine the problems with particular reference to the poor countries. The economists constructing it are working out what might be "an acceptable decent minimum welfare function which each human being should have as a birthright. And then it will ask whether the world resource situation could support such a minimum at different levels of the population." [7] Another study, being undertaken in the Netherlands, is examining whether the resources of the world could support a doubling of the world's population in twenty to forty years. This study, which is not a model, will attempt to take into account social-value factors, questions of the *quality* of life, which, since they cannot be quantified, cannot be fed into a computer. [8] When the results of these studies are known, it may be possible to make some relatively exact assessments of the revolutionary changes which confront mankind. Meanwhile, we can suggest the broad lines of these changes as possible solutions to the problems discussed in this book.

First, the basic resources of the planet—food, minerals, energy, water—will have to be regarded as "the common heritage of mankind," to be conserved and exploited in the common interest. The principle asserted for the oceans will have to be generalized. This will involve a new attitude toward the very nature of property: the ancient idea that it is a "trust" for the community—in this case, the world community—will have to replace the modern idea of absolute rights of personal or national possession.

Second, the environment, and in particular pollution, must be managed and controlled on a global scale.

Third, research and development must be concentrated with an entirely new emphasis on the problems of the poor countries, and on the global problems discussed in Chapters 17 to 20. Particular areas in which this research is needed include those of birth control and family planning, nutrition deficiency, cheap means of transporting desalinated seawater, new forms of protein foodstuffs, recycling of minerals and the development of substitutes, fusion nuclear energy and other new sources of energy, and the extraction of minerals and oil from the sea. These are but a few of the vast number of fields in which managed technology could achieve beneficial breakthroughs. Such a policy would involve altering present priorities. Instead of spending 45 percent of present research funds on military matters and 1 percent on the problems of the poor countries, the figures should be reversed.

Fourth, economic growth must be related to these three policies. The world planning policy will be basically concerned with investigating, exploiting, conserving and distributing world resources. It will therefore involve not only the international *management*—though not necessarily the ownership—of property, but the reorganization of the international monetary and trading systems.

Fifth, the overall control of growth will have to be accompanied by an overall sharing of wealth. The national welfare state, grounded on the concept of minimum incomes, will have to be extended into the world welfare state. This means that instead of attempting to bridge the gulf between the rich and the poor countries by aid, there will have to be a real redistribution of wealth, by means, perhaps, of some international taxation system, just as the national welfare state is financed out of taxation.

Sixth, disarmament is a corollary to all these policies. The huge sums spent by the rich countries today on arms could be diverted to financing the world research and development program and the world welfare state.

How are these policies to be carried out? We have already noted the comprehensive, variegated and overlapping crop of international organizations which has grown up since 1945—functional, regional, interregional and international, arched over by the United Nations. And we have seen that there is one body, a "Community," which is supranational. The way forward probably lies in five main directions.

The first is a considerable development of the untidy pattern of international bodies, especially of a functional and a regional nature— more common markets (which have already sprouted in East Africa, Central America and the Arab world), and more bodies to deal with specific tasks, such as reconstruction in Vietnam and the prevention of hijacking.

The second is the establishment of semisupranational global "communities" for matters which require global action, such as the management of the oceans, nuclear energy and the environment.

The third is the establishment of an international police force, since governments cannot be expected to surrender their right to self-protection unless they can be assured of protection by some international body.

The fourth involves some surrender of national sovereignty to a global body or bodies which would carry out global economic planning, organize the world welfare state, control the multinational corporations and direct the international peace-keeping force.

Fifth, in all these bodies, and at every level—the village, the district, the province, the nation-state, the region, the world—the concept of *participation* must be developed, so that all people are somehow actively involved. The village community will culminate in the world community. Education for world citizenship will be of key importance in this context.

The world community will not, therefore, be a neat federal structure composed of the existing nation-states. It is likely to emerge in an untidy and hand-to-mouth way, in response to particular needs; and as this process of "creeping federalism," or, to use the African word, "communitarianism" develops, the nation-state will probably just subside in importance.

Two questions may now be asked. First, what is this "quality of life"—a phrase now constantly on the lips of statesmen and in the pages of international documents—to which these objectives should be related, and which cannot be built into computer models? Second, while mankind has the means to put these policies into practice, will it have the will? If "quality" cannot be defined in quantitative terms, the ethic of the Rights of Man and the material achievements of science may need to be crowned by the spiritual insights of religion, which may also provide the inspiration to act in a communitarian way.

We suggested in Chapter 2 that the essence of religion, in premodern societies, was an awareness of "truth" through imagination, vision or revelation, and that "reason" was regarded as merely the handmaiden of these faculties. Modern man has tended to deny the validity of any kind of truth except that gained through the analytical reason. The first kind of truth is concerned with *quality*, the second with *quantity*. The great need of Western man now is to return visionary truth to its throne, but with rational truth as its partner, not its handmaiden. And here the poor countries can come—and are coming—to his aid, in three ways. First, while the Semitic religions of the West are essentially dogmatic, laying down doctrines which people are asked to *believe*, the great Oriental religions—Hinduism, Buddhism and Taoism, and the Sufi branch of Islam—are essentially mystical, offering *methods* by which the individual can gain personal *experience* of the spiritual dimension of consciousness; and this is what many people in the West are seeking. Second, the peoples of the poor countries still have living roots in their premodern cultures. Their spiritual and psychic pores have not yet been closed up by the climate of rational and secular thought which pervades the Western world. If they can retain their sensitivity to "the quality of life" in their spiritual, human and natural environments, while at the same time using Western rationalism to raise their living standards and Western humanism to sweep away degenerate social customs and codes, such as the Hindu caste system, then they will add a new dimension to the climate of world affairs. Third, many members of their elites are, of necessity, cosmopolitan personalities, blending East and West, modern and premodern, in their consciousness, and through this blending, evolving the universalist philosophies discussed in Chapter 11. Such men and women are peculiarly equipped to be moulders of the world community.

Modern man is faced with the supreme challenge to steer the growth of his global society towards a new order. He has already begun the task: in the span of a generation the foundations of world community have been laid, within the rich countries, within the poor countries, and in international structures which relate them all together. It is hard to believe that he will not now set himself to complete the edifice.

References

1. Alexander King, "The Totality of the World *Problematique* Must Now Be Addressed," in *Center Report* (Santa Barbara, California: Center for the Study of Democratic Institutions, October 1972), p. 26.

2. *Ibid.*

3. Dennis L. Meadows *et. al. The Limits to Growth* (New York, N.Y.: Universe Books, 1972), p. 43.

4. *The Observer* (London), February 11, 1972.

5. *Newsweek* Current Affairs Study, *The Future* (New York: Newsweek Education Division, May 1972), p. 9.

6. Alexander King, *op. cit.,* p. 28.

7. *Ibid.*

8. *Ibid.*

POPULATION AND PER CAPITA GNP FIGURES FOR 1973[2]

AFRICA		
Country	Population (in millions)	P.C. GNP (in $)
Nigeria	71.3	210
Egypt	35.7	250
Ethiopia	26.6	90
South Africa	24.3	1,050
Zaire	23.4	140
Sudan	17.1	130
Morocco	16.0	320
Algeria	14.7	570
Tanzania	14.0	130
Kenya	12.5	170
Uganda	10.8	150
Ghana	9.3	300
Mozambique	8.3	380
Malagasy Republic	8.3	150
Cameroon	6.2	250
Angola	5.7	490
Upper Volta	5.7	70
Rhodesia	6.0	430
Tunisia	5.5	460
Mali	5.4	70
Ivory Coast	5.9	380
Malawi	4.8	110
Zambia	4.6	430
Niger	4.4	100
Guinea	5.2	110
Senegal	4.1	280
Rwanda	4.0	70
Chad	3.9	80
Burundi	3.6	80
Somalia	3.0	80
Dahomey	2.9	110

AFRICA (*Continued*)

Country	Population (in millions)	P.C. GNP (in $)
Sierra Leone	2.8	160
Togo	2.1	180
Libya, Arab Republic of	2.2	3,530
Central African Republic	1.7	160
Liberia	1.5	310
Mauritania	1.3	200
Lesotho	1.2	100
Congo, Peoples Republic of	1.2	340
Mauritius	0.9	410
Botswana	0.6	230
Portuguese Guinea	0.5	330
Reunion	0.5	1,210
Swaziland	0.5	330
Gabon	0.5	1,310
Gambia	0.5	130
Equatorial Guinea	0.3	260

ASIA

Country	Population (in millions)	P.C. GNP (in $)
China, Peoples Republic of	811.4	270
India	582.0	120
Pakistan and Bangladesh	140.2	200
Japan	108.4	3,630
Philippines	40.2	280
Thailand	39.4	270
Korea, Republic of	33.0	400
Iran	32.1	870
Burma	29.5	80
Vietnam (North)	23.2	110
Vietnam, Republic of	19.9	160
Afghanistan	16.6	90
China, Republic of (Taiwan)	15.4	660
Korea (North)	15.0	340
Sri Lanka	13.2	120
Nepal	12.0	90
Malaysia	11.3	570
Iraq	10.4	850
Khmer Republic	7.7	130
Saudi Arabia	7.7	1,610
Syria, Arab Republic of	6.9	400
Yemen, Arab Republic of	6.2	100

ASIA (*Continued*)

Country	Population (in millions)	P.C. GNP (in $)
Hong Kong	4.2	1,430
Laos	2.9	120
Israel	3.2	3,010
Lebanon	3.0	940
Jordan	2.5	340
Singapore	2.2	1,830
Mongolia	1.4	550
Yemen, Peoples Democratic Republic of	1.6	110
Ryukyu Island	0.9	1,050
Bhutan	1.1	60
Kuwait	0.9	12,050
Oman	0.7	840
Macao	0.3	270
United Arab Emirates	0.3	11,630
Bahrain	0.2	900
Sikkim	0.2	90
Brunel	0.1	1,640
Qatar	0.2	6,040
Maldive Islands	0.1	90

EUROPE

Country	Population (in millions)	P.C. GNP (in $)
U.S.S.R.	249.8	1,790
Germany, Federal Republic of	62.0	2,930
United Kingdom	56.0	2,270
Italy	54.9	1,760
France	52.2	3,100
Turkey	38.0	310
Spain	34.7	1,020
Poland	33.4	1,400
Yugoslavia	21.0	650
Romania	20.2	930
Germany (East)	17.0	3,000
Czechoslovakia	14.6	2,870
Netherlands	13.4	4,330
Hungary	10.4	1,850
Belgium	9.8	4,560
Portugal	9.0	1,410
Greece	8.9	1,870
Bulgaria	8.6	1,590

EUROPE (*Continued*)

Country	Population (in millions)	P.C. GNP (in $)
Sweden	8.1	5,910
Austria	7.5	3,510
Switzerland	6.4	6,100
Denmark	5.0	5,210
Finland	4.7	3,600
Norway	4.0	4,660
Ireland	3.0	2,150
Albania	2.3	460
Cyprus	0.6	1,400
Luxembourg	0.4	4,940
Malta	0.3	1,060
Iceland	0.2	5,030

NORTH AND CENTRAL AMERICA

Country	Population (in millions)	P.C. GNP (in $)
United States	210.4	6,200
Mexico	56.0	890
Canada	22.1	5,450
Cuba	8.9	540
Guatemala	5.2	500
Haiti	4.5	130
Dominican Republic	4.4	520
El Salvador	3.8	350
Puerto Rico	3.0	2,180
Honduras	2.8	320
Nicaragua	2.0	540
Jamaica	2.0	990
Costa Rica	1.9	710
Panama	1.6	920
Trinidad and Tobago	1.1	1,310
Martinique	0.3	1,330
Guadeloupe	0.3	1,050
Barbados	0.2	1,000

SOUTH AMERICA

Country	Population (in millions)	P.C. GNP (in $)
Brazil	101.1	760
Argentina	24.3	1,640
Colombia	22.5	440
Peru	14.5	620
Venezuela	11.3	1,630
Chile	10.2	720

SOUTH AMERICA (*Continued*)

Country	Population (in millions)	P.C. GNP (in $)
Ecuador	6.8	380
Bolivia	5.3	230
Uruguay	3.0	950
Paraguay	2.4	410
Guyana	0.8	410
Surinam	0.4	870

OCEANIA AND INDONESIA

Country	Population (in millions)	P.C. GNP (in $)
Indonesia	124.4	130
Australia	13.1	4,350
New Zealand	3.0	3,680
Papua New Guinea	2.6	410
Portuguese Timor	0.6	130
Fiji Islands	0.6	650

References

1 International Bank for Reconstruction and Development, *World Bank Atlas of Population, Per Capita Product and Growth Rates* (Washington, D.C.: 1972).
2 Omitting certain very small territories.

INDEX